The Dentist Guide to Creating Personal and Financial Freedom

2023 Edition Fully Revised and Updated

The Dentist Guide to Creating Personal and Financial Freedom

2023 Edition Fully Revised and Updated

DR. ALBERT "ACE" GOERIG

The Dentist Guide to Creating
Personal and Financial Freedom
2023 Edition Fully Revised and Updated

by Dr. Albert "Ace" Goerig

© Copyright 2023 Dr. Albert "Ace" Goerig

ISBNs:
979-8-9880408-3-5 (softcover)
978-0-9753339-6-9 (eBook)
978-0-9753339-7-6 (audiobook)

Published by

Doctor Ace LLC

222 Lilly Rd. NE

Olympia, WA 98506

DoctorAce.com

Table of Contents

*Go to www.doctorace.com/to quickly access links to all
the online resources that are referenced in this book.*

About the Author

DR. ALBERT "ACE" GOERIG graduated from Case Western Reserve University
Dental School in 1971 and was their dis-
tinguished alumnus in 2014. He retired
from the Army Dental Corps in 1991 and
has been in private practice for 31 years in
Olympia, Washington. He completed his endodontic residency
in 1978 and became a diplomat of the American Board of endodontists in 1982. He has written numerous scientific articles on
endodontics and has contributed to three Endodontic textbooks.
He has presented at every major national dental meeting and
co-founded Endo Mastery, a coaching program for endodontists
in 1996. Through his seminars and personal coaching, he has
worked with more than 22% of all endodontists and their teams
in the United States and Canada. He continues to see patients
twice a week in a fun and effortless practice.

In 2004, he wrote his first book: *Time and Money: Your
Guide to Personal and Financial Freedom*. His newest book,
entitled: *The How-To Book Of Dividend Growth Investing—Create
Generational Wealth and Passive Income for Life!* was published
in March 2023 and is available on Amazon. He has a free website,

www.doctorace.com with audios and videos to help individuals quickly become debt-free and understand dividend investing. Dr. Goerig and his wife, Nancy, have been married for more than 53 years and have 5 children and 14 grandchildren.

Preface

AS DENTISTS, WE HAVE ONE OF the greatest professions, and, as Americans, we live in one of the greatest countries in the world with all the opportunities to have a life of our dreams. Yet many dentists have yet to find happiness and contentment in their practice and their lives. One problem is that we were not taught in dental school the secrets of creating a great, fun, and profitable practice. Nor do we have enough education or understanding about personal finance and investing. We think we will get rich through investing, but many dentists lose money by placing it into several various so-called investments that they know nothing about, such as unnecessary standard whole life insurance policies, risky stocks and speculative real estate, hedge funds, commodities, day trading, and limited partnerships, hoping they will strike it rich.

We forget that the real money is made in our practice, and the best investment we can make is to pay off our debts first before we invest anywhere. Paying off debt is investing and gives you the maximum guaranteed return without any risk. We need to learn to love what we do and focus on creating a practice that is fun and profitable. My mentor, Kendrick Mercer, taught me that "Life is a process, not an end; if you don't enjoy the process, you'll hate the end!" This book is about learning to enjoy the process.

Through this simple and specific guide, you will be able to increase your practice profitability, pay off debts quickly, and reach financial freedom while you savor and enjoy every precious moment of your life to the fullest. In this book, I will show you the most efficient way to become financially free by using the two vehicles that can get you a guaranteed, risk-free 100% return on your money. Using this approach, most doctors could be debt-free in 3 to 5 years and financially free in 10 years. You will learn how to enjoy work more while creating an incredible relationship with your patients, team and family. The rewards are many. But most of all, I urge you to enjoy the process.

Dr. Albert C. (Ace) Goerig
Olympia, Washington
March 2023

Foreword

YOU ARE ABOUT TO MAKE THE MOST important decision of your life. This process will begin when you realize that your past does not define your future. You have the power to write a new personal and financial story. This journey begins when you delve into Ace Goerig's seven secrets for creating personal and financial freedom for dentists.

I have known Ace for decades as a friend. I've also followed his career as a super-successful endodontist and one of the best coaches I know. His newest book has the power to become the guide through the financial minefields of myths and mistakes where dentists find themselves during their careers. Make no mistake: waiting until you are in your 50s or later is exactly the wrong strategy for a safe, secure financial future. All of us should strive for a future with a variety of choices and options in our lives, which we can secure by the actions and decisions we make today. The scary part of this realization is that most doctors don't realize their mistakes until it is too late. When it comes to eliminating debt and saving money, starting as soon as possible is fundamental. As with most things in life, there is never going to be perfect timing or a perfect situation. The secret is just starting where you are, now. I have had the honor to speak to thousands of dentists every year, and the one thing that I find they share is a lack of understanding of the basics of debt and financial freedom. This misunderstanding or lack of knowledge is the fundamental element in every doctor's struggles. Learn to control consumption debt, and you'll set into motion a lifetime of predictable wealth building.

For most of us, the struggle begins with the misunderstanding that debt is normal and unavoidable. Generations of people have assumed that they will always be in debt, and that it is OK. But nothing could be further from the truth. Ace will give you real-life examples of his staff members and friends who have bucked the trend and decided to re-write their stories. He has created a guide that has been found "tried and true" thousands of times. You are fortunate that you don't have to reinvent the wheel or spend one more day struggling, only to find another strategy that does not work. Ace outlines a concise, consistent financial plan for dentists, a playbook for success in life that works.

Michael Abernathy, DDS
National speaker and founder of Summit Practice Solutions
Celina, Texas

Chapter 1

Creating A Beautiful Story

IN A MAY 2017 INTERVIEW with Charlie Rose, Warren Buffett was asked what gave him his greatest joy. "I love going to the office," said Buffett. "It has been my painting for more than 50 years: I get to paint what I want, and I own the brush, and I own the canvas, and the canvas is unlimited. And that is a pretty nice game, and I get to do it every day with people I like. I don't have to associate with anyone that causes my stomach to turn. If I were in politics, I'd have to smile at a lot of people I want to hit. I've got a really good deal, and I am hanging onto it."

Most dentist-owners forget that they have the brush and the canvas, and they can create their story any way they want. Sometimes it takes the insight of a coach to help them through the process.

CREATING A BEAUTIFUL STORY

We are here on this planet for a relatively brief period, and all we have is from now until the end of our lives. So, how can we make the most of this time? To live our lives to the fullest, we need to create a new vision or story of what is possible. We all can live the rest of our lives as a very exciting adventure. For most of us, because of our cultural context and the lack of training we have received regarding financial matters, it is difficult to set up a guide for reaching financial freedom, or even to recognize that our way of relating to money could be very different. However, if we write a story about how we want to live, it is easy to develop and follow a guide to fulfill that story. But most of us don't know how to develop a coherent and compelling story about financial and personal freedom.

I was raised poor by a single mom. I had a 2.3 GPA in high school and was only accepted into college only because I'd set the state pole-vaulting record. I spent three years studying Engineering, and the Army ROTC taught me how to fly fixed-wing aircraft so I could fly helicopters in Vietnam in 1966. Instead, in 1965, I met my cousin, who was a dentist, and he recommended that I go to dental school.

I changed majors and graduated from dental school 6 years later. I then spent 20 years in the Army as a Dental Corps officer. During that time, my family and I moved 12 times, had many different assignments, and really saw the world from a unique perspective. Life became an incredible story for me. The fun is in always developing new stories, so after I retired from the Army, I began a new story, and after a difficult start, I created a very successful dental practice. Eventually I developed a dental-consulting company to share my story with other dentists who were struggling, just as I had, so I could help them create a beautiful story for their own practice and lives.

The best stories are specific and flexible—specific in offering a full vision with rich detail, and flexible because life is a process, and we are always growing. As new experiences arise, we begin to see things at a deeper level. When situations change, we need to give ourselves permission to change our minds to stay within our own integrity. You can create a beautiful story that incorporates abundance into your life.

Having your finances in order will help support your positive story so you can live life fully. However, writing a life story takes great courage because it involves change. Sometimes you need to change many things to live a free and independent life. In this case, you are called upon to face your fears of confrontation and conflict to create the life you want. Your story shows the world your intent to change and starts you on your new path. Gandhi was once asked, "What is your message to the world?" He replied, "My life is my message." What is your message to your children?

HOW TO BRING ABUNDANCE INTO YOUR LIFE

The reason we create positive stories is to let the universe know what we want. I personally believe that we can bring anything—positive or negative—into our lives depending on our thoughts. This happens by creating a clear, positive vision of exactly what we want and know (believe) that it will come about. This could be an increase in referrals, doing more cases, finding the right associate or team member. Over 100 years ago, in his book, *The Science of Getting Rich*, Wallace Wattles talked about focusing on what you want and not what you don't want in your life. We need to put our energies into the creative and not the competitive aspects of life.

I never spend any time worrying about what the other dentist is doing. Why? Because there is unlimited abundance, if we have the right focus and vision, we can bring whatever we want into our lives. The real fun is helping others create abundance in their lives. I spend little time listening to the negative events in the news which I cannot control. The real joy and happiness comes from relationships with family and in my practice. Abundance always comes when we are thankful for all the gifts and richness that we have in our lives.

MY NINETY-YEAR-OLD MILLENNIAL STORY: RETIRE IN PRACTICE

As members of the Baby Boomer generation, most of us were taught to work hard, put in the hours, take three weeks' vacation a year, and retire after 40 years of practice to play golf and enjoy the sunsets. Yet many dentists still work after age 65, not because they want to, but because they have to, due to poor management of money, or because they have had too many "successful" marriages.

We look down upon the millennials because they seem to be more interested in enjoying life now, taking more time for themselves and their families, and are not as concerned with money as we Baby Boomers were. Yet down deep, those two generations are more alike than not. Because of our cultural imprinting, we did not know that we could write a better story. Both generations see the possibility. Let me tell you about my ninety-year-old millennial.

When I first came to Olympia, Washington, as an endodontist in 1991, one of my favorite referring dentists came in for a root canal. He was in his 70s yet looked like he was in his 40s. I commented on how great he looked, and I asked him what his secret was. He told me he had "retired in practice" only 10 years out of dental school.

In the 1950s, when he had graduated, most dentists worked 5 days a week and took about 2 weeks' vacation a year. After a year in practice, his classmate told him that he could really work 4 days a week if he just modified his schedule, and he could make just as much money and have more time off. He did, and it worked. He told me he and his wife were not big spenders, so they were able to pay off the mortgage on their house and on the practice debt within 10 years of graduation.

After that, he realized he needed to work only 3 days a week. He started taking more vacations each year to be with his family, enjoy his hobbies, take continuing-education courses, and to relax and be much more creative in the way he ran the practice. He paid his team on salary, so they also had time off. He eventually retired at age 82 and enjoyed his very long and loving marriage. He came by my office in his early 90s and showed me pictures of himself skiing on the top of Mount Rainier with his great-grandson and fly-fishing with his daughter. He recently passed away, shortly after his wife died. I am sure he enjoyed his millennial-style life.

What most of us do not realize is that we, too, can enjoy this retire-in-practice story (more specifics on how to retire in practice in Part Five). We just need to create it, and, in dentistry, we can. We can do this by getting out of debt as soon as possible, and by creating a practice that we love that is profitable and fun. Benjamin Franklin retired from business at age 46 to have more time to work on other interests and to contribute to the well-being of society while creating a personal legacy. What will be your legacy?

Don't do stupid things with money. The main mistake dentists make is living beyond their means right out of school and burying themselves in debt. Instead, know that you will have plenty of money to get out of debt quickly. Once you are debt-free, learn to invest consistently and safely on your own in a secure environment and you will never worry about money again. With the right guide, this is all possible, and that is what I will show you in this book.

The Great American Scam consists of monthly debt payments and has changed the American Dream into a nightmare. We are lulled into a false sense of security and ownership. The banks have trained (fooled) us to stay in debt our whole lives through credit cards, mortgages, refinancing, and other loans, while they take from us two-thirds of our life's earnings in monthly debt payments. Unfortunately, most dentists do not understand how our money system really works.

A TALE OF TWO DENTISTS

Let's compare the tales of two 25-year-old dentists.

Dentist A earns $200,000 a year. He has fallen for the scam and lives big. He buys the big practice, big home, expensive cars, and other toys to build ego and find happiness while continually creating debt and making monthly payments. He has no money for practice consultants.

After 30 years, he has paid off his mortgage, practice, and school loan, but at age 55, he still has a second mortgage, car payments, credit cards, timeshare payments, and other debts, and only $225,000 in savings.

He resents going to work because he is working to pay off debt and not for the relationships or the fun of it. This creates poor relationships with his family, patients, and team.

He will give to his creditors two-thirds of his life's earnings, including the taxes he has paid on that income. Along with that, he will have given up his freedom and a life of choice, which will keep him working for many more years because he has to—not because he wants to.

Dentist B also earns $200,000 a year. However, Dentist B lives simply, like a student, and she learns how to be profitable in dentistry, allowing her to pay off all debts, including credit cards, car, mortgage, school loans, and practice debt in 10 years. She brings in a practice-management consultant, who helps her increase her net profit to $450,000 a year. Over the next few years, she will increase her yearly net to more than $800,000.

At age 35, she has no debt, has retired in practice, and now works because she wants to, not because she has to. She loves going to the office three days a week, with 8 to 12 weeks off a year for vacation to be with her family and friends. She now has 60% to 70% of this income to invest for retirement, children's education, travel, or charitable contributions.

She has an associate, and the office is open 5 days a week. Even though she works only 120 days a year, she will earn more than Dentist A, except she will go to the office for the relationships and the fun, not because she needs the money. She now has the time to expand her relationships, enjoy other pursuits, and even make a difference in her community and the world. At age 55, she will have been debt-free for 20 years, and, because of her increase in net profit, her net worth is more than $7,000,000.

YOU CAN BECOME A MILLIONAIRE

Here are the lessons from the book *The Millionaire Next Door*, by Thomas Stanley and William Danko. Wealth is not the same as your income. Wealth is what you accumulate (net worth) and not what you spend. Wealth comes from hard work, dedication, planning, and self-discipline. Millionaires do not live in upscale neighborhoods or drive fancy cars. A millionaire's goal is to become financially independent, which is much more important than displaying high social status. These financially successful people control their consumption and do not allocate too much money to products and services.

Millionaires are frugal and not only live below their means, but they also live *well* below their means. Most millionaires live in an average home, drive a used car, and their children go to public schools. They are married to the same spouse, who is also a conservative spender. Warren Buffett, one of the richest men in the world, has lived in the same modest house for more than 50 years, sent his children to public schools, and drives an 8-year-old car.

We all have choices on where we want to spend our money. We could buy a smaller house, go on fewer vacations, buy a smaller car, or put more money in investments. Most people do not consciously sit down and consider their choices, but, instead, they do haphazardly spend their money without focus. Until we are debt-free, we are restrained by our income, so we need to create a game plan and focus our excess money to draw a guide of personal and financial success.

WRITING YOUR OWN STORY

Most dentists I work with want to have more time off to enjoy their family, hobbies, and personal time. Many of them are burdened by long-term debt, are stressed at work, and exhausted when they come home. They are unable to see the possibilities that life and their profession has to offer. Before they create the life, they have to first imagine it. With the right vision and game plan, they could be debt-free within 2 to 7 years, work 3 or 4 days a week in a drama-free, stress-free office with the people they like. Once debt-free, they could take 6 to 10 weeks' vacation a year and have plenty of time to be with and create incredible relationships with family.

So, whether you are a practice owner or an associate, you have the canvas, and you have the brush to create the life of your dreams. This book was created for you, to show you the possibilities in your practice and personal life, and give you the tools and ideas to create your story. As you go through the book, write down the things you want to change in your life and the steps that you will take to create your new life story. The possibilities are endless.

Chapter 2

The Fastest Way to Become Financially Free

WHEN PUTTING ALL INVESTMENTS in perspective, the best returns are from paying off debt and increasing your practice profitability. These choices can give you a return of more than 100%. Below are the past 10 years' average returns on various investments.

- **Home:** 0–5%. According to Zillow, while home prices have appreciated nationally at an average annual rate between 3% and 5%, depending on the index used for the calculation, home-value appreciation in different metro areas can appreciate at markedly different rates than the national average. Over time, home values grew about 0% after inflation. Plan on spending 5% of the value of the home to buy it, 10% to sell it, and 1% to 2% a year to maintain it.

- **Average actively managed fund investment:** 2.6%. According to Forbes, the average investor in a blend of equities and fixed-income mutual funds has earned only a 2.6% or less net annualized rate of return for the 10-year period.

- **Inflation:** The average-inflation rate reported by the U.S. Department of Labor for the United States is 2.8%. In 2022 we saw that rate increase up to 9%. This significantly reduced the return on a 2% bond by 6%.

- **Short-Term Bonds:** Over the past 5 years, bonds have returned only 1.4% annually. Currently they are returning 5% as of February 2023.

- **S&P 500:** The historical average yearly return of the S&P 500 is 10.345% over the last 100 years, as of end of January 2023. This assumes dividends are reinvested. Dividends account for about 40% of the total gain over this period. Adjusted for inflation, the 100-year average return (including dividends) is 7.214%

- **No-fee investing:** Paying no fees on your investments results in getting you up to 70% more on your investments. Paying 1% to 4% in fees to financial advisors, brokers, or mutual-fund companies that actively manage your investments could cost you 70% of your return, making you work 10 to 15 years longer before you can retire. If you pay fees of 3% and your investments return only 4%, you got 25% of the return, and your broker and mutual fund got 75% of the return. What happens when the return is only 2%? Your commissioned broker's mantra is "Heads I win, tails you lose." Learn to invest on your own. This book will show you how.

- **Routine practice-fee increases:** Can produce a 10% to 30% increase in net profit.

- **Paying off debt:** Up to 1000% (10x) return.

- **Dental practice-management consulting:** Up to 1000% (10x) increase on return of investment over time.

Most of your advisors will not appreciate these numbers because each of them looks through a different lens, based on their experience and training, and each of them will have a different agenda for you and your money. Your banker's motivation is to get your money into their bank, so they can loan it back to you. Your CPA gets paid to do your state and federal income tax and keep you out of tax difficulty. Because most accountants do not understand business and are risk-averse, their advice would be not to do coaching because they cannot understand the benefits, and they see it as just an expense.

Surprisingly, some CPAs are concerned that an increase in your net income would increase your taxes and that would be a bad thing. Your investment advisor will encourage you to put your money into your investments and a 401K plan, so they can continue to receive fees. When it comes to your money, you are the only one who cares more about it than any of your advisors.

You will see how the power of paying off debt can give you a guaranteed return of 100% to more than 1000%, without risk or tax consequence. Many owner/dentists could significantly improve their net profit 100% in one year by bringing in a competent consultant. This is magnified to more than 1000% in 10 years.

Everyone needs to focus on what investment of your time and money produces the greatest returns. If you execute the last four strategies correctly, you will have more money than you will ever need, which you can trade in for time, freedom, and choices. The market becomes a place to compound some of your excess money. I will show you the best strategies to safely get the best returns by yourself, without paying the extraordinarily high fees and commissions of financial advisors and brokers.

Once debt-free, a dentist would be able to maintain her/his lifestyle, fund their retirement, and need to work only three days a week, and still take off 8 to 12 weeks a year, which I call "retire-in-practice." They could create a beautiful story and environment for themselves and their teams, and love going to the office knowing they have plenty of time off to play. Under those circumstances, why would you ever want to retire?

When this strategy is implemented correctly, you will have created an automatic investment program through high-dividend-producing companies, and you will not worry about the ups and downs of the market. Knowing that you are in for the long run and will not sell, eventually you can live off all the dividends of these funds. Remember that increasing the productivity of your practice and paying off all debt first, before investing in the market, will safely provide the highest returns with much more predictability.

FREEDOM FACTS

The fastest way to become financially free is to pay off all debts before you put money anywhere else. The advantages to paying off debt first are:

1. Easiest and simplest to do and understand.

2. Can make more than 100% return on your money, guar- anteed, without risk or tax consequence.

3. Can be done automatically, right out of your bank account.

4. Changes you from a spender into a saver.

5. You can now invest more into higher-return stocks like the S&P 500 index fund because your paid-off home acts like a long-term inflation-adjusted bond. The 20% of your income that you were using to pay off your mortgage now becomes a bond-like investment, getting 20% return on your paid-off home.

6. Once debt-free, you have three times the amount of disposable income (previously, two thirds of your disposable income was paid toward debt) to spend on investments and enjoying life.

One of the biggest misconceptions that keeps you in debt that is perpetuated by banks and accountants is that you should not pay off your house early because when you have a mortgage, you can write off the interest rate on your taxes. This allows the banks to continue to get a large amount of interest from you using your money. If you are in the 28% federal income tax bracket, itemize your deductions and pay one dollar of mortgage interest, and save $.28 in taxes. This means you lose $.72 of the one dollar to save $.28 taxes.

Let's look at this closely: in 2023 an average American couple who pays $10,000 a year in interest on their home loan has the choice of either taking the standard deduction of $24,000 or itemizing their return and taking the $10,000 tax write-off. When they itemize, they are unable to take the standard deduction of $24,000 and have an overall loss of $14,000 in standard deduction. The biggest loss is in the interest you paid the bank, which could range to more than 200%.

Please consider a $310,000 mortgage at 4.5% for 30 years. Below, you can see that, of the first year's loan payment of $18,849, only $5,001 goes to principal, but $13,848 goes to interest, which is lost forever to you. See Figure 1 below. This is a 277% loan, not a 4.5% loan.

In the 28% tax bracket, you had to earn around $17,724 and pay taxes on that to get the $13,847 to give to the bank as interest payments, which makes it a 354% loan. If you had paid an additional principal payment of $5,230.75, you would have eliminated one year's payment and saved $13,617.95 in interest and made 354% return on your money, guaranteed, without risk or any tax consequence.

Year	Interest	Principal	Balance
2023	$13,848	$5,001	$304,999
2024	$13,618	$5,231	$299,768
2025	$13,378	$5,471	$294,297
2026	$13,126	$5,722	$288,575
2027	$12,863	$5,985	$282,590
Total (after 5 years)	$68,833	$27,410	$282,590

The reality: over the next five years, you would have paid $96,243 in loan payments and only $27,410 would have gone to pay off the loan. You must understand that the interest is always the highest at the beginning of the loan, and for the first ten years of a 30-year loan the interest paid will always be more than 100%. Always take advantage of this guaranteed high return. The bottom line: you invested $5001 and made $13,848, which is a guaranteed 277% return without risk. With this great return, why would anyone not use the money in their savings (only earning less than 1%) to pay off their home? You should also cash out any non-tax-deferred stocks and pay off debts.

When we have debt, saving money is an encoded trap that keeps us poor. In the above example, if we have $100,000 in your savings or non-tax-deferred investments the best, safest, and highest return on that money is to pay off debt. Paying $100,000 toward the $310,000 home mortgage would drop your mortgage to $210,000 and save you $121,360 in interest payments while paying off 13 years of the mortgage.

Compare this $121,360 made by paying off debt to the $1,500 you would get with an after-tax return of 1.5% in a 2% bank CD on that same $100,000. You must see the $100,000 put into the house as a high return, safe, long-term inflation-adjusted bond that is always available to you through lines of credit or second mortgages. Once the home is paid off, the money used for mortgage payments becomes a constant source of available cash flow. It is like getting money from a bond. Remember, focus on paying off debt before you put your money anywhere else. Once you are debt-free, I will show you specific investment strategies that provide safe and predictable results. Most people can be debt-free within five to ten years using this guide.

Below are two excel charts that show exactly how much interest you are paying over a certain period of years.

30 year - $300,000 loan - Real interest rates before and after taxes (24% federal, 6% state tax)									
	At the 30 year		At the 20 Year		At the 15 year		At the 10 year		At the 5 year	
		Real rate		Real rate		Real rate		Real rate		Real rate
Interest rate	Real rate	before taxes	Real rate	before taxes	Real rate	before taxes	Real rate	before taxes	Real rate	before taxes
3.50%	181%	258%	105%	150%	72%	103%	45%	64%	21%	31%
4%	225%	322%	127%	182%	86%	123%	52%	75%	25%	35%
5%	337%	481%	179%	255%	117%	167%	69%	99%	32%	45%
6%	486%	694%	242%	346%	153%	219%	88%	126%	39%	56%
7%	686%	980%	319%	456%	196%	280%	109%	155%	47%	67%
8%	954%	1363%	414%	592%	245%	350%	132%	188%	56%	79%

	30 years		20 Years		15 years		10 years		5 years	
Interest rate	interest	principal	interest	principal	interest	principal	interest	principal	interest	principal
3.50%	$10,408	$5,757	$ 8,280	$7,885	$ 6,774	$9,391	$ 4,981	$11,184	$2,846	$13,320
4%	$11,904	$5,283	$ 9,619	$7,568	$ 7,947	$9,240	$ 5,904	$11,282	$3,411	$13,776
5%	$14,899	$4,426	$12,391	$6,935	$10,425	$8,900	$ 7,904	$11,422	$4,667	$14,659
6%	$17,900	$3,684	$15,270	$6,313	$13,068	$8,516	$10,097	$11,486	$6,090	$15,494
7%	$20,903	$3,047	$18,239	$5,711	$15,854	$8,097	$12,473	$11,478	$7,679	$16,272
8%	$23,909	$2,506	$21,279	$5,136	$18,763	$7,652	$15,015	$11,401	$9,430	$16,985

DEBT IS THE DEVIL

It's all about net worth. Our net worth is the total of all our assets, including our investments, bank accounts, and real estate, minus our debts. Paying off debt increases your net worth (wealth) and provides an asset that you can use in emergencies as loan collateral. Paying off debt is a conservative investment strategy.

So don't be happy about having more tax deductions, especially when you can't write them off due to the high standard deduction. This is how the government and the banks keep you in debt and in servitude.

There is no good debt, only bad debt. All debt is bad, bad, bad! Debt keeps you imprisoned and prevents you from living a life of freedom, independence, and choice. Being overburdened with financial responsibilities increases your stress and can damage important and satisfying personal relationships and even lead to divorce, which could cost half of what you own. By changing your spending and saving habits one step at a time, you can regain control of your life. You now know what interest payments really cost you and what to do to change your spending habits.

In John Cummuta's excellent audiobook and manual, *Transforming Debt into Wealth*, he states, "Every time you make a purchase on credit, you need to consider not just the price you're paying for the product, but the price plus interest plus how much that money could have earned you as an investment."

U.S. households now owe $13.15 trillion in total debt, and about $931 billion of that is credit-card debt, according to NerdWallet's 2017 American Household Credit Card Debt Study, along with its newly issued quarterly figures. In 2017, the average family's collective balance on all credit cards was more than $16,000. If the family makes just the minimum payment, it will take them 37 1/2 years to pay off the balance; over that time, they will make total payments of more than $43,000, of which $26,000 would be interest. This is just as if someone said to you, "I will lend you $16,000, and you will pay me back $43,000." If you were to invest the same $26,000 in an individual retirement account (IRA), it would grow to $284,329 over 30 years at 8% interest. We have spent tomorrow's money already and are making payments on it.

With each debt, the interest you pay puts you on the wrong side of the compound-interest equation. It's important to realize that you are going to make a finite amount of money in your life. If you give too much of it away in interest payments and impulse buying, there will not be enough money left over for you to retire comfortably. You can take two basic approaches with your money: you can spend it on things that don't add meaning to your life and stay in debt and eat cat food in your retirement years, or you can build your financial future now by paying off debt early and retire early in style.

Every dollar you consume now brings you one dollar of value, but every dollar you invest for your future can bring you 5 to 20 times that amount in your retirement years, allowing you to retire 10 to 20 years earlier. Reducing spending and paying off debt will eliminate your money problems and improve your relationships. It will also improve your health by reducing stress. And it will serve as a shining example for your children about what is possible.

How would it feel to be out of debt and own your home free and clear, with utilities, taxes, and food as your only real expenses? This is possible for everyone if they're following a clear guide. Most people can pay off all their credit-card debt in one year and their car in the second year. By the third year, they're making extra payments toward their mortgage. Most doctors can be totally debt-free within 5 to 10 years and thereby eliminate payments on student loans, home loans, and practice debts.

When you become debt-free, there is no need to worry about your credit report because you pay cash for all your purchases.

The ability to obtain credit is what got you into trouble in the first place. The idea that you need to build up your credit by borrowing is an illusion that keeps you in debt. Once you become debt-free, no one owns you, and this is true freedom.

HOW TO MAKE 1,000% INTEREST

Interest rates for dental-school loans can average anywhere from 6% to 8% per year. Look at an actual 30-year, $300,000 dental-school loan with an interest rate of 7.9%, for which the doctor pays $2,180 per month. During the first year of repayment, only $2,556 goes to principal, and $23,608 goes to interest. The doctor must earn around $30,000 and pay tax on those earnings, to cover that amount of interest each year. This is more than 1000% interest. When determining how much student loan you will need, remember that, for every $1000 you borrow, initially, you will have to pay $10,000 in interest back to the bank which does nothing to pay back the loan.

Year	Interest	Principal	Balance
2019	$23,609	$2,556	$297,444
2020	$23,399	$2,766	$294,678
2021	$23,173	$2,992	$291,686
2022	$22,928	$3,237	$288,449
2023	$22,662	$3,503	$284,946
Total (after 5 years)	$115,771	$15,054	$284,946

In this example, by making one additional principal payment of $2,766 that year, you will eliminate (save) $23,399 that you will never have to earn and give the bank, allowing you to make more than 1000% return on your money. This is a no-brainer.

Where else can you get 1000% return on your money, guaranteed, without risk? All those dentists who have student loans must focus on paying off this debt quickly—especially those who are paying high interest rates. If you paid an additional $3,888 per month, your payment would be $6,068 and you would pay the loan off in five years, thus saving $420,835, or about $550,000 before taxes. This is the best deal ever. The reality: If you decided not to pay off the loan in five years, then during those five years, you would pay $130,825 in payments and only $15,054 would go to pay off the original loan amount.

STEPS TO ELIMINATE DEBT FOR THE DOCTOR AND TEAM

Eliminating debt is a crucial first step in my guide. The only debt that is reasonable to incur is for the purchase of very large items such as your house, your education, your practice, or your car. Never go into debt for anything else, especially not for consumable items such as vacations.

I can't state it any more clearly: consumption debt is bad, bad, bad, and bad. The best guide is to spend less than you make and to save a substantial amount of your money. Then you can consume with saved dollars. Most families in America are imprinted to use their credit cards and consume, whether they have the money to pay for something or not. When you do this, you typically pay high interest rates; this is not an effective way to manage your money. Instead of a credit card, use a debit card. This way, you pay as you go, and you eliminate interest payments. For a step-by-step approach to eliminating debt quickly, go to Doctorace.com.

CREATING A DEBT-FREE OFFICE

Early in my private-practice career, I had a 401K plan and even a defined benefit plan. Because the plan was managed by financial advisors and brokers who invested into actively managed funds, the returns were dismal compared to the S&P 500 index fund. Most of my returns went to pay fees to my advisor and the mutual-fund company. I also noticed that, when people left my practice, they would immediately cash in their retirement plan and spend it on something stupid.

Because the returns were so poor with my old plans, I decided to eliminate the retirement plans completely, and give each team member a $250 per month debt-reduction bonus. Even now, each year around the Christmas bonus time, I have a dinner meeting with my entire team and their spouses, and show them how quickly they can be debt-free using the snowball approach as described in Doctorace.com. I also encourage them to go to Dave Ramsey's financial peace university, and, once they complete the program, I will pay for the tuition. For other doctors who want to help their team get out of debt, I have included the entire audio and video program on my website: DoctorAce.com.

This has been in effect for more than 6 years, I have 4 team members now completely debt-free, and most of my team are now paying off their homes. I have faith that they will be completely debt-free within 6 to 10 years.

But my greatest gift to them is not being out of debt; my greatest gift is that I changed them from spenders into savers. This has done much to eliminate the money issues that many families argue about. Here is an example of one of those team members.

LISA'S STORY

Her husband was making about $15 an hour on his physically demanding construction job. They decided to live on his income and focus everything she earned from their eBay business and her salary from my dental office toward debt reduction and paying off their houses. They owned 2 homes, and, within 4 years, they had paid off their mortgage, sold one of the homes, and invested the profits into her company. Once debt-free, they can maximize the Roth IRA and create a simple or 401K plan for her side eBay business, put in $30,000 per year, and at age 65 will have $10,600,000 in their 401K Roth receiving a passive income of $300,000 per year.

Lisa has since left my dental practice. She and her husband work about 15 to 20 hours a week on their eBay business and have plenty of time for travel and enjoying the adventures of life. They had their first child in November. It is surprising how, with strong intent, becoming debt-free happens very quickly.

HERE IS HOW TO ELIMINATE ALL DEBT IN THREE TO FIVE YEARS

Here is how to quickly pay off your debt. The average American dentist takes home around $200,000 a year. Most doctors live on $150,000, which gives them $50,000 per year to pay off debt. But the following chapters also describe how to become more profitable and/or use a dental practice-management consultant to increase your income by $160,000 a year by just doing one additional large procedure per day, such as a crown. If your crown fee is $1,000 and you work 200 days a year, doing an additional crown every day would bring in $200,000 each year. After paying lab fees and materials on the $200,000, you will have made an extra $160,000 from the crowns.

After paying taxes on the $160,000, you will still have an extra $120,000 each year to pay toward reducing debt. Add that to $50,000 of your original disposable income, and you will have $170,000 to pay off debt. One more crown a day will give you an extra $14,166 each month to pay off debt.

Once you are debt-free, you have that additional $14,166 plus your monthly payments of $10,127, equaling $24,293 per month ($291,596 per year) available for investing and your lifestyle. If you invested $250,000 a year in dividend-growth stocks, you could have $18,493,000 in 20 years and be receiving $559,000 per year in passive income. This is called freedom.

Chapter 3

Becoming More Profitable in Your Practice

YOUR PRACTICE IS YOUR economic engine, so optimize it to the fullest. You can make more money in your practice by creating efficient systems, providing top-notch customer service, plus a loving and incredible team, high efficiency, and beautiful clinical results.

In 1991, I retired from the U.S. Army after serving 20 years, including 12 moves and multiple job duties from general dentist, endodontist, endodontic resident mentor, and clinic chief, to commanding officer of a dental command. I was from the state of Washington, so when I retired, I just drove south from Seattle until I ran out of traffic and found the beautiful town of Olympia, which needed an endodontist.

A little afraid of opening my practice, I started in a small, three-operatory, 600-square-foot office that another dentist had just left. At that time, I knew very little about opening a practice and had no practice-management ideas, so I brought in a local dental consultant to help me set up my systems. She was very helpful, and we implemented systems and hired three assistants and one office administrator.

Being one of only three endodontists for a population area of 200,000, I was swamped with patients, and I was working 5 days a week, 10- to 12-hour days, killing myself and my team. What I did not understand was how to schedule patients properly, which resulted in excessive stress and very low production.

After the first year, I was exhausted and wondered if I should have just retired from dentistry completely. There was a lot of complaining and drama from my overworked team. Some days I would drive up to the office and think that I should maybe just keep on driving. One Sunday, I came into the office and was going through the front desk drawers and noticed a lot of bills that had not been paid, and checks that had not been deposited. It turned out that the woman up front was overwhelmed with her duties but had not told me.

Eventually, I realized I was nine months behind in payroll taxes, my life insurance had been canceled, and I was $250,000 in accounts receivable over 120 days because I did not know we needed to collect at the time of service, and she did not know we needed to send out statements. We were basically living on insurance payments.

Because I had lectured nationally, I knew most of the great practice-management coaches on the circuit, and the best coach I knew was Linda Miles. I hired her to come in and turn my practice around. She was incredible and taught me the importance of real systems, such as scheduling, marketing, and creating a superior team.

I also learned how to use practice monitors and know the numbers I needed to track, including understanding my profit and loss (P&L) statement. I hired a local bookkeeper to teach me how to use QuickBooks. I did my own QuickBooks for six months to better understand my overhead expenses and learn the ins and outs of QuickBooks. Then I hired the same local bookkeeper to come to my home office twice a month and enter all of my personal and business numbers from my checkbook and credit-card statements into QuickBooks.

He also balances my checkbook and prints out all checks, including refunds. Each quarter he does my 941 federal tax return, state unemployment and state disability taxes, and city taxes. I also had him set up QuickBooks $500-a-year payroll accounting program. This saved me from working with a payroll service at $2000 a year, and it was much easier for my office manager to put in payroll hours. I pay my bookkeeper $36 an hour and last year paid him $1,900 for my business and $600 for my personal accounting. He has a great knowledge of taxes and works very closely with my CPA. I have an excellent CPA who oversees everything, gives me advice, and does my tax returns for around $7,000 per year. She is very responsive, up to date and thorough; she understands the IRS codes and makes me follow the rules.

I review the profit and loss statement and office production monitors monthly. You need to have good practice monitors which you can obtain from one of your fellow dentists or a dental management coach. When you understand and monitor the numbers, there is less chance of embezzlement (staff-initiated bonus), an unfortunate but always real possibility.

A two-doctor general dentistry practice in my town was embezzled for $1.9 million over seven years, and it can happen to you if you don't know your numbers. We hired new employees and an experienced administrative team member. I reduced the number of patients I saw, focused on enjoying each individual patient and the dentistry, and even got home on time. Within a month, I was much more profitable, doing procedures I loved.

Since that time, I've had many different practice-management consultants come into my office, and every time it has been of great value. I have always had an interest in the business of dentistry and will share with you that I have learned from these consultants. I have been fortunate to be in one of the best dental communities in the country, where dentists are open to sharing and helping other new dentists in our community. Many of the ideas that I'm sharing with you come from my dental consultants, from the dentists in my local community, and from what I have observed in their practices.

The annual collections for the average dental office in the United States is around $700,000 with an overhead of around 69%, resulting in a net of $220,000 for the doctor. In this chapter you will find many strategies to increase profitability and reduce your time in the office. Below are four successful practice models of some of the best general practitioners I know.

Note that the doctor has an empowered team to run the office, which allows the doctor to have 98% of his or her time to focus on direct patient care. The office has a minimum number of employees to reach high production goals. Each of these offices used a practice consultant to improve efficiency and double profitability. With increased profitability, it does not take a practice long to become debt-free, thus resulting in personal freedom and many more life choices.

SUCCESSFUL PRACTICE MODELS

Dr. K. Classic 2/2/2 model. This is a mature dental practice with two administrative staff, two dental assistants, and two hygienists. They all work four 8-hour days (32 hours) per week (185 days a year) with 6 weeks of vacation. The doctor is very efficient, highly skilled, and a great communicator with his patients. He focuses on high-quality restorative treatment and refers most of his periodontics, endo, and oral surgery out to local specialists, which further increases his efficiency. The team provides superior service to their patients and understands how to create an emotional connection with each patient. Dr. K collects $1.4 million per year with a 50% overhead, resulting in a $700,000 net profit. Remember that 80% above your base overhead is net profit.

Dr. M. 2/2/2/1 model. This is an owner/doctor in her 40s with one associate. There are 2 administrative staff, 3 dental assistants and 2 hygienists. The team works four eight-hour days (32 hours) per week. The owner/doctor works 3 days a week (125 days per year), and the associate works 2 days a week (90 days per year) compared to the average dentist who works 195 days per year. The doctor is very efficient, highly skilled, and a great communicator with her patients. The practice has an excellent team that leads and manages the associate. They collect $1.9 million per year with a 68% overhead, resulting in a $600,000 net profit for the owner/doctor. This is also a retire-in-practice model.

Dr. H. 1/1/1 model. This model includes Dr. H. plus one administrative member, one assistant and one hygienist. They work four 10-hour days (40 hours) per week (180 days a year) with 6 weeks of vacation. The doctor is efficient, highly skilled, communicates well with patients, and has an excellent team. He collects $1.2 million per year with a 50% overhead, resulting in a $600,000 net profit. He believes that the extra 8 hours per week (of which 80% is net profit) significantly increases his bottom line as compared to most offices that work only 32 hours.

Dr. R. (retired in practice) 1/1/1 model. Dr. R.'s practice includes one administrative member, one assistant, and one hygienist. They all work three 9-hour days (27 hours) per week (125 days a year) and all take 10 to 12 weeks of vacation. The team is paid on salary. The doctor is very skilled in dentistry and communication, and is efficient, with an excel- lent team. He collects $700,000 per year with a 50% overhead, resulting in a $350,000 net profit. He has been debt-free for years and has a strong base of patients who continually refer new patients to him.

Each of the above dentists got out of debt quickly and invested in dividend growth blue-chip stocks as described in this book. Each became financially free in their early fifties.

CREATING THE OFFICE CULTURE

The action of writing your vision is the most powerful way to make your new story happen. Once written and shared with the team, it becomes the culture of the practice. When writing about your new vision, think about the movie *Jerry McGuire* and check out the YouTube video "Jerry Maguire Mission Statement."

Write a vision statement describing how you want your practice to be. This process will start you thinking about what is important to you in your practice as you create your office culture. A vision shows the world your intent to change and starts you on your new path. A vision makes a strong statement to the world about who you are and where you are going. It is like a magnet that will bring into your life all the ideas, people, and tools you need to make it happen. It is also like a compass on a ship: it allows the captain to sail in a specific direction and helps guide the changes he needs to make to get to his new destination. Below is my own office vision statement, which I placed at the front office, where all patients can see.

My Office Vision: We are in a continual process of creating a story for our practice that is both fun and exciting and brings each of us personal fulfillment, joy, peace, and freedom. Through dedicated people, ideas, and the use of systems, we will develop a positive, nurturing, and safe environment to grow and fulfill our needs both personally and professionally. It will be a place of mutual respect, laughter, clear communication, and teamwork in an atmosphere that is fun, energized, and joyous. We will connect with our patients on a personal level and provide a patient "Wow" experience that it is so incredible that they will hesitate to leave our office for fear of entering a harsher world. Our office will have a reputation of high-quality treatment, being so gentle, safe, and caring that we will receive many new referrals from our existing patients. We will enjoy every day to the fullest and live in each moment. Our office will be filled with laughter, pride, a sense of ease, and a calmness that allows us to provide to each patient an experience that is unsurpassed.

CREATING AN EFFICIENT OFFICE

Most dentists waste two to four hours a day in unproductive procedures that take too long and do not even pay the overhead. Many spend too much time on a poorly designed schedule doing small-case, average procedures. Too much time is lost on the phone or computer, on team-management issues, or just talking too much. Many doctors think that improving their techniques or getting new equipment will increase their net profit, but the 90% of real profitability is in efficient office systems and training the team to run those systems. Dentists must learn to do dentistry and empower the team to manage the practice, so the doctor can stop spending extra hours on practice management. If you empower your team to run your practice, you need only three to four hours per month for practice management.

Many dentists try to coach themselves and go to practice-management seminars and then come back and try to train the team to change their systems. The problem is, they don't know which systems to change. That's why it is essential to have an on-site consultant observe office flow and the quality of the team members, and then evaluate which systems can be improved and which systems need to be changed. The dentist/ owner needs to let go of any members of the team who cause unnecessary drama and frustration to the doctor and other team members. When the systems really flow well, patients love being in the office, the team loves serving the patients, and the dentist loves doing the dentistry. This whole process can be a lot of fun for everyone.

IDEAS AND SYSTEMS THAT CAN DOUBLE YOUR NET PROFIT

- **Phone and scheduling skills.** Today, most dentists feel they just don't have enough patient flow and believe they need to spend more time on external marketing. They could easily double their patient flow using effective phone skills with new patients. One of the best companies to help train your team on customer service and phone skills is All-Star Dental Academy. (https://www.allstardentalacademy.com/).

   Not only does All-Star have outstanding training programs that ensure new patients come in for an appointment, but it also teaches your team superior customer service. The scheduling module is excellent, and All-Star now has a program on how to present (sell) the dentistry, all for just a few hundred per month.

- **Presenting and selling dentistry.** You have the greatest case acceptance when you have a doctor, team, and culture that can create an emotional connection with the patient. Because most dentists are uncomfortable presenting treatment plans and fees, this is best done through well-trained and incentivized hygienists.

- **Increasing internal referrals.** If you are not growing, you are not doing everything to inspire your patients to refer. Low-intensity referral is from 0 to 12 new patients per month. When you get below 10 new patients per month, it probably means you are offending them. When you get 13 to 25, that is normal; 26 to forty is good, and above that is excellent. If you're getting 40 new patients a month and you are not growing, the problem is not consumerism, but capacity, which is space, equipment, staff, and doctor's speed. It takes only one of these factors to be substandard to bring the practice to a halt.

  With high-intensity referral, of 25 to 40 new patients a month, patients are initiating the referrals. These are patients who call their friends just to tell them how incredible their dental visit was. When you obtain this level of referral intensity, you will draw patients from your entire area. Remember that 80% of your profitability comes from 20% of your patients. These are the patients who pay on time, appreciate you and your team, sing your praises, and have friends just like them. Focus your internal marketing on those patients.

  How do you achieve true referral intensity? Patients love to find great value and share that with friends. If your patients get what they expect, then you're in the middle zone. If they get more than they expect, then you move to the highest level of referral intensity. Go through the office and rate each step of the patient experience as low, average, or high. Any phone calls must be gracious and encouraging. When patients come to the office, they should be greeted by the person they talked with on the phone.

Referral negotiation is best facilitated by the team rather than by the doctor, and the following script must be delivered exactly (note that it is important to employ pauses long enough for the patient to focus on what you're saying).

Before treatment: Mrs. Jones, can I ask a favor? (Pause) If we can really impress you with how you're treated today, would you do something for us? (Pause; wait for the answer. Once they agree, continue.) If we can really impress you with how you're treated today, would you send us your friends, your family, and the people you work with? (Then wait for them to respond.)

After treatment: How did we do? Were you impressed? (When they say "yes," give them a couple of cards with some type of discount or offer printed on the back, so they can distribute them to their friends.)

Creating an emotional connection with the patient: This begins with your first phone call with the patient, which is more about listening than talking. Each team member and the doctor need to be trained to ask more questions about the patient and talk less about themselves, so we listen and talk with the patient focus coming from your heart.

Sometimes, we get very fearful of patients because of their poor past dental experiences. Before I meet the patient, my assistant tells me that the patient is very nervous, so when I come into the room and introduce myself, I tell them that I am very gentle. I will sit face-to-face with them and address their fears. I remind them that those fears from the past are embedded in their subconscious so they have no control of the fear when they come into the office.

I also tell them that it takes great courage to face their fears and show up. Because of their courage, I promise them three things: I will always get them completely numb, they will always be in control, and I am very fast and efficient in my treatment delivery. This helps put the patient immediately at ease. Then getting to know the patient is fun. Here is a thank-you note from one of my patients that demonstrates the importance of emotional connection.

"Dear Dr. Goerig, two weeks ago, I got a diagnosis of breast cancer stage IV. Two days after that I woke up with a swollen cheek and learned I needed a root canal and ended up in your chair. I was still emotionally reeling from my health news but noticed the poster from your time at Fort Knox, Kentucky. I was stationed there as an Army dietitian and, when I shared all my story, you were so gracious, compassionate, and funny that you helped me relax and almost enjoy my time in your chair. Thank you for letting God use you to minister to me and reassure me of his love and care. You may not have been aware of it, but you were my angel that day! I still tear up thinking about it, how you verbally encouraged me, loved me, encouraged me further, and then even reduced my charges, so I would not be facing such a huge bill. You are an angel, and I can't thank you enough for being the conduit of God's love to me that day. I really needed it and won't ever forget it. God bless you and your whole family. With gratitude."

- **Same-day service.** There is another practice hidden within your practice. If you have a practice that schedules $75,000 per month, there is another $75,000 hiding in same-day service. The hygienist reminds patients of a condition that has already been diagnosed or just found and asks them if they would like to do the treatment that day. Case acceptance is far higher with same-day service. Once your office embraces the idea of same-day service as a normal part of doing treatment, handling the finances is not a problem. We only incentivize same-day service that is highly productive ($700 or higher) and that we want to do.

The bonus for the person who gets a patient to say "yes" is $10, and the bonus for the assistant is $5. Same-day service is the secret to a high case average. When you try to sell harder on the first appointment, you can drive patients away from your practice. When case average (total practice production divided by all new patients) rises above $2,500, referrals go down. When case average rises due to same-day service, referrals may rise at the same time. Low case average usually means high volume, which means more staff, more overhead, and lower profitability.

- **Bonus system.** When I was in the Army for 20 years, I would work very hard for three years in an assignment to get a $0.10 ribbon. This same incentive doesn't work as well in civilian life, but showing your appreciation through bonuses and thanking them often does pay big dividends. One of the most effective ways to increase profitability is to implement a smart and effective bonus system that can motivate your team while it increases your net profit.

  To make a bonus effective, everyone on the team must understand how the bonus is calculated. It is much better to give bonuses on a daily or monthly basis instead of yearly. That way, you get much more excitement and participation from the team. Bonuses should be designed to reward the entire team, not just individuals, although individuals can be rewarded for making same-day service work or for increasing case acceptance.

All bonuses must be based on collections, with the understanding that total team compensation should not exceed 20%. Large purchases should not be added to average overhead expenses when considering this 20%. When you are trying to help your team get out of debt, remind them that bonuses can accelerate their debt reduction.

There are many types of bonus systems out there, and I would highly recommend that you work with a practice consultant who will help you implement a bonus structure that works best for you in your practice. I feel the best and most immediate bonus that you can give your team is to compliment them and thank them often for specific things, such as filling the schedule properly, creating great relationships with your patients, and making same-day service work. Individually, I thank each of my team players for being part of our incredible team.

- **Adult oral-sedation dentistry:** Fear of dentistry is one of the main reasons that only 65% of the population go to a dentist. Many of those with the greatest fears have extensive dental work that needs to be done. Becoming certified in adult oral sedation will help you take better care of your fearful patients and is available for those patients who would like to have extensive work done all at one time under sedation.

The best course for dentists is provided by DOCS education. It is by far one of the best courses I have ever taken. They also have an IV-sedation certification course. https://www.docseducation.com 855-227-6505

Those who truly want a lifestyle practice have learned to drop most dental insurances. All-Star dental practice management helps many practices drop their dental insurances and become fee for service; to help them do that, many create practice membership. In this model, the patient pays a certain amount each year, such as $150 to $197 per person, which includes a 10% to 15% discount on all the dentistry during the membership year. For this membership, you provide an exam, X-rays, and two cleanings per year (you can knock off $20 for children).

You can offer to upgrade patients to this program once they need dental treatment. Membership patients are usually uninsured but can be offered discounts to encourage large treatment plans. Some states are trying to restrict practice-membership plans due to the pressures of dental-insurance companies; check with your state.

Focus on the dentistry that is less stressful and more profitable. Focus on and become extremely efficient on the 20% of the dentistry that gives you 80% of your profit. It always seems that the most profitable and successful dentists in town refer out a lot of their specialty work. The average profitable dentist in our area collects around $800,000 and takes home only $300,000 net.

One of my best referrals learned from the prosthodontist how to use very sharp diamonds to do incredible, beautiful crown preparations in 5 to 10 minutes. This doctor collects about $1.5 million per year and takes home around $750,000 net. This is because he focuses on the procedures he does efficiently and less stressfully and refers out the rest. The reason for the high net is that most of the collections above $800,000 go to net profit.

He once told me that the greatest enemies of the general dentist are difficult patients, stressful procedures, and unpredictability. That is why he refers most of his endodontics and other nonrestorative treatments out to specialists. I have personally found that the most profitable dentists in my community have strong professional relationships with the specialists.

DEVELOP A WIN-WIN RELATIONSHIP WITH YOUR SPECIALIST

- Specialists help you to be more profitable by allowing you to refer those cases that are stressful and not profitable and instead to focus on the dentistry you do best. They are a resource for you to expand your knowledge and can help and support you with difficulties in treatment. They are a second opinion and support your treatment plan. I also like to tell referred patients what a great office and dentist they are coming from during my treatments. Specialists also can be a source of referrals. And one thing that is often overlooked is, the more we share, the more abundance comes into our lives.

IDEAS ON HOW TO IMPROVE SPEED AND QUALITY

- **During the day, have your dental assistants time you.** If you are taking too long on various procedures, such as molar root canals, get additional training or refer out to a specialist. Ask your local supply rep for the name of the best and most respected dentist in town, and ask the local lab owner which dentist does the most crown work with the highest quality. Call the doctor and ask if you can observe them in their office. You may want to video the procedure. Ask if you can bring your chief clinical assistant and front-office team member to observe the flow of the practice. Buy lunch for the doctor's team. Meet with the doctor for dinner and ask if he or she will mentor you. All great dentists are always looking for someone they can teach. Get involved in local study clubs.

- **Add new profitable services to your practice** and learn to master them. Such services may include Invisalign or dental sleep medicine that focuses on the use of oral appliance therapy to treat sleep-disordered breathing, including snoring and obstructive sleep apnea (OSA).

- **Buy the patient records from another practice** when that dentist is retiring.

- **The office should be a place of safety and peace for the entire team.** Fire all employees who create drama in your practice. You cannot change people, but you can change people.

- **Handling clinical or office frustrations.** When things are not going exactly the way you want, don't get upset, just laugh. Or you can use the following words to refocus and stay on task: great, next, isn't that interesting, or it is what it is. Frustration and anger are detrimental to obtaining high-quality clinical results and creating a fun and profitable office.

- **An updated, superior website.** This is one of the first places a referred patient will go to check you out. It must have good photos, good information, and testimonials from your patients. It should be designed so that your website on your phone looks exactly like it does on the computer. It should have a patient review area and a testimonial section. It is a good idea to have these testimonials moving across the page, so that, when a patient looks at their phone, they see the testimonials. One of the best web-design companies for dentists is PBHS.com.

- **Addressing negative family and cultural imprints about success.** Many dentists do stupid things with money because they have no formal training in understanding financial matters. But the biggest issues are the imprints and cultural beliefs about money that we learned from our family.

    Some examples are: you have to work hard to earn money; getting rich is a matter of luck; money is the root of all evil; when things are going good, they will always go bad. You may have felt unworthy as a child, and this imprint prevents you from being successful and profitable in your practice, thus causing you to sabotage your own success in practice and your investments. One of the hardest things I need to do, as a coach, is to help clients get past their low deserve level that is embedded in their subconscious and prevents them from becoming more profitable and happier in their lives. This is also true when investing their money.

The purpose of this book is to provide a simplified investment game plan that keeps my clients away from financial advisors, risky investments, and other situations where they would lose their money. I knew one doctor who continued to self-sabotage in his investments and practice. He fortunately got a great dental coach, who helped him create a highly profitable practice, and he was finally able to put enough money away so he could retire. After he sold his practice and retired, he had all the money he needed to enjoy a fun and exciting retirement. Unfortunately, his inner demons took over again, and he invested all his earnings from the practice into a real-estate deal where he lost it all. For those doctors who continually self-sabotage and do stupid things with money: you may find yourself living on your Social Security in your children's home and taking vacations in a 200-mile radius.

If you have poverty consciousness imprinting or a low deserve level, you need to get professional help to break your behavioral patterns around money. One company that has helped many of my coaching clients is Legacy Life Consulting at https://www. legacylifeconsulting.com/. They will help you address the issues that cause you these problems and help you understand prosperity consciousness. With their help, you can create a story that allows you to expand your life and move out of your old comfort zone.

- **Become a stronger leader.** The owner/doctor is the source and responsible for writing the vision based on his or her core values, which create the culture of the practice. Leaders must be authentic and trust in themselves, always learning and open to all possibilities and willing to accept change. When you are not leading and paying attention, there will be much more drama in the team because they have lost respect for you. Great leaders empower their team to lead, but each senior team member knows the vision and direction of the practice is coming from the doctor.

Doctors will sometimes give up the leadership role because they're trying to be nice and they do not like conflict. But when the doctor gives up the leadership role, someone will step in to take over that role. When you get clear and want to step back into the leadership role, you will get pushback from the person who has led the team, and they will resent you because it appears you did not appreciate their efforts. This may end up in the dismissal of that great employee. Great leaders win hearts before minds. Read Simon Sinek's book *Start with Why: How Great Leaders Inspire Everyone to Act*. Here are a few ways to keep growing as a leader:

☐ Give up control, delegate, and empower the team.
☐ Get out of the way, but follow up.
☐ Know the numbers (use practice monitors).
☐ Spend 98% of your time in direct patient care.
☐ Lead by example, and be the best employee.
☐ Tell the team what you want.

• **Small practice changes result in enormous increases in net profit.** It is amazing how an increase of just one more crown a day (by doing same-day service) can affect your net profitability. Look at the chart below. One more crown per day increased the net profit by 181%, from $197,647 to $357,647, resulting in a net annual income increase of $160,000. If you did two additional crowns per day, you would realize an extra $320,000 in increased net income. With this extra $320,000 per year, your entire school loan debt, home, and practice loan could be paid off in five to six years. Once you are debt-free, you will have three times the amount of money to be able to work less, invest, and enjoy your personal freedom. This is all possible if you are open to new ideas and dental coaching.

	One More Crown per day		Average Dentists	
	Amount	%	Amount	%
Collections	$802,583	100%	$602,583	100%
Overhead	$444,935	39%	$404,935	67.2%
Net profit	$357,648	61%	$197,647	32.8%
Daily collections	$4,013/day		$3,012/day	
Monthly collections	$66,881/month		$50,215/month	
4 days/week worked	200 days/year with two weeks off			

The best dental practice-management book written is by Michael Abernathy, DDS entitled: *The Super General Dental Practice: Everything Is About to Change.* You're about to discover how to transform into the practice you never thought possible. To get a free copy of the book, go to: http://www.supergeneral-practice.com

Here are a few great websites for practice-management ideas. Each of these also offers practice-management coaching.

https://www.allstardentalacademy.com/
https://blatchford.com/category/podcast/
https://summitpracticesolutions.com/
https://www.whitehallmgt.com/ https://growingyourdent-albusiness.com/

RAISE YOUR FEES ANNUALLY

MANY DENTISTS DO NOT get around to raising their fees annually or semiannually. I recommend that you routinely raise your fees 2% to 4% a year just to keep up with inflation and the rising cost of dental materials. Even though you are locked in by some insurance plans, you should routinely do this for all other patients.

Most owners do not understand the power of raising fees to increase net profit. If you have a $100,000 per-month practice and your overhead is 70%, your net profit would be $30,000 that month. A 10% increase in fees would give you an additional $10,000, when added to your net of $30,000, you would have a total net of $40,000. This is a 33% increase in your profit.

Below is a chart that shows you how a 1%, 3% and 5% increase could affect the total net income of your practice over 30 years. Go to ADA.org/feesurvey to get a free 2023 fee guide for your area. These are free for ADA members.

You can also purchase the updated fee guide for your ZIP Code from Wasserman-medical.com for $169. Try to keep fees that the patients call about in the 80th percentile. Because of dental-insurance companies pressures, you cannot collaborate to set fees with other dentists, but you can ask them what their fee guide is and then make your own decision regarding what your new fees will be. You may also hire someone to negotiate your fees with your insurance companies. (Check out Becky Balok at www.bbdentalconsulting.com.)

Increased Net Profit by Increasing Fees

Totals	Yearly Collections	Total Collections Increase		
		1% per year	3% per year	5% per year
30 years	$500,000	$2,556,370	$9,501,339	$19,880,395
30 years	$1 million	$5,112,740	$19,002,678	$39,760,790
30 years	$1.5 million	$7,669,110	$28,504,017	$59,641,185

HIRE A PRACTICE-MANAGEMENT EXPERT

WHY WOULD ANYONE WANT to spend the money to bring in a dental consultant? The main reason, of course, is that what you're doing right now is not working. Doing more of it just becomes frustrating and exhausting. I think the big reason many dentists resist is that they are afraid to give up control of the practice or that it might not work.

Many dentists have never taken the time to set up an efficient business model. To significantly increase practice profitability, hire a coach who is familiar with your type of practice (that may include areas such as sleep apnea, conscious sedation, Cerec crowns, etc.) or who has a good track record of success. Just by modifying a few things in a practice, dentists can often double their net profit. Remember, adding just one more crown per day increases your net profit by more than $200,000 a year. Having systems in place to schedule patients more efficiently, doing same-day service, collecting fees at the time of service, emphasizing more profitable procedures, and raising fees are all examples of best practices that significantly increase the bottom line without raising overhead.

Most dental consultants can modify your business model, so you work three or four days a week instead of five and take four to eight weeks off each year for vacation. Profitability increases to a point where the doctor can pay off all debt within three to seven years. This is accomplished through systems and creating an incredible story: retiring in practice. With this model, why would anyone ever want to retire?

Dentistry is changing rapidly, and many forces are causing stress. Some of the external forces over which we have no control are: more corporate offices, increasing overhead due to insurance companies controlling fee growth, more general dentists, fewer dentists retiring, and the big one—money spent on retail shopping, vacations, and timeshares instead of maintenance dentistry. We need to learn to stop stressing over things we cannot control and focus on what we can control.

Things we can control are internal factors such as low production, doctor compensation, fewer patients, tougher cases, open schedules, no-shows, last-minute cancellations, student debt, office drama, and overwhelming administrative challenges. If your practice is not growing, it is declining. More than 70% of all practices declined over the past few years.

Many dentists are frustrated and stressed in their practice. They think attending a practice-management course will help them clear these problems. The real problem is that they don't know what is wrong and what they can really fix. Many have already spent too many hours trying to control their practice. The most important service a practice-management coach can provide is to determine those issues that are holding you back and help you correct the systems and team issues that plague your practice. This why the consultant must come to the office for a day to speak with the team and observe the office flow and schedule.

Most dental students pay more than $100,000 a year for their education, which does not include anything about practice management or efficient systems. Yet they balk at paying a consultant $50,000 a year to change the practice and become much more profitable. They see the consultant's fee as an expense and not an investment. But in fact, your practice is the engine of your life where your money is made, and a lot of dentists' engines need to be repaired or tuned up. A good dental consultant can maximize the efficiency of that engine, resulting in two times or more increase in your net profit.

I have a different practice-management consultant come in to my office every three to four years, and it has always resulted in increased profitability. Many of these companies will do a free objective analysis of your practice and help you understand where improvement is needed.

Here are few I recommend: https://blatchford.com/; https://summitpracticesolutions.com/; https://www.whitehallmgt.com/, and All-Star Dental Academy (https://www.allstar dental academy.com/).

I have personally worked with each of these companies in my own practice and can highly recommend them. If you are interested in a consultant, I would interview each of them to determine which company would be best for your practice. Coaching can result in an increase in monthly collections of $100,000 to $250,000 a year and more. And 75% to 80% of that increased collection is net profit. Once the practice's systems are changed and you increase your collections, it is rare to backslide. So, even conservatively, that one-time investment of $50,000 can result in an increase in collections of $1 million to $2.5 million over the span of 10 years. This is why a practice consultant is called "an investment."

More importantly, the doctor who uses a consultant is finally creating a practice that he or she loves, with an A-team and happy, enthusiastic patients and high profitability. Implementing the most successful coaching, the doctors can increase their vacation time by an additional two to four weeks a year and still increase productivity. Remember that Uncle Sam pays 35% to 50% of the consulting fee; if you have a partner, you also split the investment with him or her. Most doctors pay off a consultant's fee in the first three to six months with increased collections. The two questions you must ask yourself after trying to change all the issues in your practice are, "How is what I am doing now working?" and "What is the true value of time with my family and time for myself?" Consulting helps you get peace of mind and your freedom.

When you're looking for a consultant, I would initially check with your friends and the most successful practices in your dental community who have used coaches and ask them how good their experience was and most importantly, what the result was from their coaching process. When selecting a consultant, it is important that you have a compatible philosophy of practice and that the consultant understands your needs and concerns.

Make sure any consultant you consider uses online monitors to help you understand and track your important numbers, and monitor your progress. You must be clear about your own goals and believe that the consultant's philosophy will fit you and your team. So, give yourself permission to be your best, and to reach your and your team's full potential.

WHAT DO YOU LOOK FOR IN A CONSULTANT?

- Has significant experience working in a dental office

- Has significant experience working as a consultant

- Can show you a track record of results

- Can give you three to four references from dentists they have coached

- Understands your problems and gives you insights and suggestions

- Can help you become a better leader and help you give up control

- Has an extremely positive personality, not negative or condescending, and can create a strong working and teaching relationship with your team and team leaders

- Understands the numbers (and can teach you how to understand the numbers)

- Offers a program that is individualized, not cookie-cutter

- Comes to your office so there is no loss in your production time

Very few dentists see coaching as an investment that can give them a more-than 1000% return. Many more will sign up for help when they have enough pain. One famous quote was, "When the pain to remain the same exceeded the fear to change." If you are not ready to be open to new systems, be able to let go of control and empower your team, unable to fire a bad employee, or think you already know the answers, then you are not ready for coaching. Working with a coach requires the willingness to implement positive change for both you and your team. If you can face your fears and are open to change, the rewards are many. The greatest reward is your freedom in your personal and professional life. Transform your practice and you transform your life.

USE A CONSULTANT TO HELP YOU CREATE A RETIRE-IN-PRACTICE MODEL

In our culture, retirement has somewhat of a negative connotation indicating old age, too old to work, or a reward for working hard for 40 years. I do not buy into this antiquated concept of retirement. By my definition, retirement is the time of many choices, opportunities, and excitement. I believe you can begin your retirement when you're young through the concept of "retire in practice." This happens when you become debt-free, which allows you to have unlimited choices for your life, even in your thirties, forties and fifties.

One of those choices is to work one day less a week, thus allowing you to spend more time with your family when you are young. Another choice is to take more time off for travel, to teach, to create or enjoy your hobbies, or work on your bucket list. Ask yourself what the message is that you are sending to your children about how to live life. Give them the example, throughout your life, of what real retirement (choices) looks like. A good consultant can show you how to increase your profitability, get out of debt early, and work fewer days. They can also help you bring in an associate when the time is right.

Even though your practice is a constant source of income and can allow you to work as many days as you want, there may be a time when you are debt-free and financially free and would just like to sell your practice, work one or two days a week, or just walk away. There is no right answer, but you do have choices and the time to figure out what works best for you. You and your spouse need to create this story together.

Retiring in practice begins with a beautiful vision, the right systems, scheduling, great team, efficient techniques, and marketing. Once you totally become debt-free, which happens much sooner when you have increased your practice profitability, you can bring in an associate without reducing your net profit. Hire a doctor who wants to be a long-term associate and does not want to have any of the issues involved with running a practice or ownership. They must be compatible with you and have your same treatment philosophy.

You can now drop to three days a week, be open five days with an associate and take much more vacation time because your practice is covered. When you work fewer days, you are refreshed, use higher-quality treatment, and enjoy your practice more. You create an empowered team that runs the practice, but you maintain complete control. Re-program your belief that you need to work hard. Be and live healthy while creating the adventure of your life.

Instead of selling your practice, bring in another associate and come into the office four hours per month, just to check in with the team and review the numbers. This is called the retire-out-of-practice model. You can take home half of your previous net without doing dentistry.

To do this you need an empowered team that runs the practice while providing an ideal patient experience through loyal associate doctors and motivated team members. To maximize the practice's success, work with a practice-management consultant each year to ensure that all systems are monitored, new team members are trained, and office leaders are supported to enable the doctor's goals to be met. Below is a chart of the retire-in- and retire-out-of-practice model.

Chapter 4

Achieving Financial Freedom

*The problem in America isn't so much
what people don't know; the problem is what
people think they know that just isn't so.*
—Will Rogers

EVERYTHING YOU HAVE BEEN TAUGHT about money makes other people wealthy and keeps you poor. Creating wealth is not complicated! The secret to become financially free is to make more money in your practice, quickly pay off debt receiving a guaranteed tax-free return, and then learn how to maximize your personal investments in a tax-free environment.

These options are never offered to you by your financial advisors because no one makes money off them. What you are offered are risky stocks and mutual funds with high commissions and advisory fees, along with the high anxiety associated with these products. The other supposedly safe type of investment are low-return bonds or treasuries that will never provide adequate passive income for your life.

Most of your advisors will not appreciate this paradigm shift because each of them looks through a different lens based on their experience, training, and what they will make from you. Each has a different agenda for you and your money. You need to create your own agenda that works best for you.

Over the past 50 years, Americans have been taught by banks, the government, financial advisors, and financial institutions to stay in debt while telling them that the only way to become wealthy and retire comfortably is to accept risk, volatility, and unpredictability in the stock-market casino through 401K plans and other financial vehicles that they control.

These investment models will take away two-thirds of your disposable income and freedom while keeping you broke, unable to retire, and in debt for the rest of your life. You become their cash cow until you die. This book will help you learn a simple, safe, and predictable system to create wealth, obtain your personal and financial freedom and leave a legacy for your family.

You will learn how to be completely debt-free in 3 to 7 years. I will show you the best strategies to safely get the best returns for yourself, without paying the extraordinarily high fees and commissions of financial advisors and brokers. You'll learn how to invest in the stock market while taking minimal risk simply and safely.

THE COST OF ADVISORS

Below is a real example of an actively managed mutual-fund SIMPLE IRA compared to the results of the S&P 500 fund over the last 12 years. In this true example, the individual would have had $636,159 rather than $320,000 (almost twice as much) if they would have just put their investments in the S&P 500 ETF (exchange traded fund).

YEAR	BROKERAGE ACCOUNT			RETURNS		S&P 500 ACCOUNT			RETURNS	
	$ OPEN BAL	$ DEPOSITS	$ PRINCIPAL	%	$	$ OPEN BAL	$ DEPOSITS	$ PRINCIPAL	% PRETAX	$ TREATED
2009	0	7,800	7,800	-0.81%	-63		7,800	7,800	26.46%	2,064
2010	7,737	14,950	22,687	5.98%	1,357	9,864	14,950	24,814	15.06%	3,737
2011	24,044	15,400	39,444	-2.44%	-963	28,551	15,400	43,951	2.11%	927
2012	38,481	14,950	53,431	9.99%	5,339	44,878	14,950	59,828	16.00%	9,573
2013	58,770	15,600	74,370	8.56%	6,368	69,401	15,600	85,001	32.39%	27,532
2014	80,738	15,750	96,488	2.86%	2,761	112,532	15,750	128,282	13.69%	17,562
2015	99,249	15,600	114,849	-4.34%	-4,984	145,844	15,600	161,444	1.38%	2,228
2016	109,865	16,900	126,765	6.95%	8,807	163,672	16,900	180,572	11.96%	21,596
2017	135,572	18,650	154,222	12.64%	19,499	202,169	18,650	220,819	21.83%	48,205
2018	173,721	15,654	189,375	-7.26%	-13,751	269,023	15,654	284,677	-4.38%	-12,469
2019	175,624	17,046	192,670	16.67%	32,112	272,209	17,046	289,255	31.49%	91,086
2020	224,782	19,520	244,302	11.24%	27,449	380,341	19,520	399,861	18.40%	73,574
2021	271,751	20,822	292,573	9.37%	27,427	473,435	20,822	494,257	28.71%	141,901
2022	320,000		320,000			636,158		636,158		

Below is another real example of a much larger office, with nine employees, that has maximized all tax-deductible strategies. These are two identical plans except one has just invested on their own in the S&P 500, compared to the investment of their financial advisor and brokerage company. They would have had more than $7 million in their 401K account instead of $2.8 million. This office lost $4,226,867 by using their financial advisors to manage their portfolio through mutual-fund investments.

YEAR	BROKERAGE ACCOUNT			RETURNS		S&P 500 ACCOUNT			RETURNS	
	$ OPEN BAL	$ DEPOSITS	$ PRINCIPAL	%	$	$ OPEN BAL	$ DEPOSITS	$ PRINCIPAL	% PRETAX	$ TREATED
2009	479,897	80,000	559,897	9.81%	54,926	479,897	80,000	559,897	26.46%	148,149
2010	614,823	86,175	700,998	9.55%	66,922	708,046	86,175	794,221	15.06%	119,610
2011	767,920	86,001	853,921	-0.61%	-5,250	913,830	86,001	999,831	2.11%	21,096
2012	848,671	85,443	934,114	9.51%	88,826	1,020,928	85,443	1,106,371	16.00%	177,019
2013	1,022,940	85,673	1,108,613	10.07%	111,585	1,283,390	85,673	1,369,063	32.39%	443,440
2014	1,220,198	80,179	1,300,377	2.94%	38,289	1,812,503	80,179	1,892,682	13.69%	259,108
2015	1,338,666	81,850	1,420,516	-10.66%	-151,461	2,151,790	81,850	2,233,640	1.38%	30,824
2016	1,269,055	87,873	1,356,928	8.48%	115,049	2,264,464	87,873	2,352,337	11.96%	281,340
2017	1,471,977	88,238	1,560,215	10.13%	158,112	2,633,677	88,238	2,721,915	21.83%	594,194
2018	1,718,327	94,982	1,813,309	-6.73%	-122,059	3,316,109	94,982	3,411,091	-4.38%	-149,406
2019	1,691,250	98,899	1,790,149	12.52%	224,184	3,261,685	98,899	3,360,584	31.49%	1,058,248
2020	2,014,333	96,245	2,110,578	11.93%	251,810	4,418,832	96,245	4,515,077	18.40%	830,774
2021	2,362,388	116,383	2,478,771	13.10%	324,803	5,345,851	116,383	5,462,234	28.71%	1,568,207
2022	2,803,574		2,803,574			7,030,441		7,030,441		

I highly recommend that anyone who has a 401K plan should do a comparison **now** and not wait until they're ready to retire. On my website, I have a free Excel comparison worksheet to see how your investments have done compared to the S&P 500 fund. You can also just go to https://www.efast.dol.gov/5500search/ and put in your EIN number to get copies of past 5500. This will show you the beginning balance and contributions you put in each year. Use these numbers to fill out the chart. This will help you realize how much you have lost or gained in your retirement account by using the various advisors and mutual funds.

Free S&P comparison Excel calculator at https://www.doctorace.com/resources/

If you find that your advisors have done poorly compared to the S&P 500, you need to transfer your portfolio into an account that you have control of and about which you can make your own investment decisions. The how-to book on dividend-growth investing will show you step by step how to identify, select, and purchase the best dividend-growth stocks.

Most of my clients open a Charles Schwab IRA or 401K account and transfer their funds into that account. This way, they can self-direct their investments and teach their team to do the same. If you are an Endo Mastery client, we help you through this process.

I am now a big fan of 401Ks because of the most recent Secure 2.0 Act 2, which was passed in late 2022. This will allow you to maximize your Roth portion of the 401K. The average dentist and spouse can put in as much as $100,000 into their 401K yearly. Anytime that you can maximize the Roth portion of any investment, you should do so. I would rather pay tax on $1,000,000 now instead of the tax on $20 million 20 years later in the highest tax bracket.

The late John Bogle, father of the indexed mutual fund, said in MarketWatch: "If you pay a hefty fee to an active manager, what happens to your potential return? Answer: Nothing good. At 2.5% over a typical investor's lifetime, an astounding 80% of compounding returns end up in the hands of the manager, not the investor's."

Fees of only 1% per year can slash the value of your savings by 28% over the next 35 years, according to the Department of

Labor. These are in addition to other fees in actively managed funds such as trading costs, taxes, and hidden fees.

Most individual investors put their money in mutual funds and rely upon money managers, financial advisors, and brokers who engage in hyperactive trading to try to beat the market by picking winners and timing. This is a losing strategy. In most cases, investors would be better off consistently investing on their own in a S&P 500 index fund (SCHX or SPY).

Bogle believes in index funds and says actively managed funds are a big scam. When you invest in loaded, actively managed mutual funds, you put up 100% of the capital and take 100% of the risk. If you make money, your fund manager takes up to 70% or more of the upside in fees. If you lose money, they still get paid. They are charging you 10 to 30 times what it would cost for you to buy a low-cost index fund that would match the market and beat 90% of the actively managed mutual funds.

Expenses and fees are the enemy of the individual investor. You must understand that advisors, brokers, and mutual-fund managers are well-meaning salespeople. They charge 1% to 4% of your entire portfolio even when you lose money. They will take 50% to 80% of your gains.

If you invest on your own in an index S&P 500 fund $4,000 per month for 30 years at 7% return, you will earn $3,781,475. What will your financial advisors and mutual fund take from your earnings when they charge only 1%, 2%, 3% or 4% fees?

Advisory/Fund % fee	The money Advisory/ Fund will take from you	% Return of your earnings
1%	$962,322	25%
2%	$1,725,989	46%
3%	$2,332,220	62%
4%	$2,820,600	75%

As you can see in the chart above, they will take from you up to 75% of your earnings. They will get their fees even when you lose money that year.

> *"Unfortunately, the vast majority of those who bill themselves as financial advisors neither charge a fair price nor give good advice. More than any other market I know, the market for financial advice is 'Let the buyer beware.'"*
> — Jim Dahle, M.D.

Remember, the person who cares the most about your money is you. Learn to invest on your own, and stay away from financial advisors and brokers who work on commission.

> *"You must unlearn what you have learned."*
> — Yoda

As Yoda taught in *Star Wars*, the first step is letting go of how you have been programmed in the past. This guide shows you a simple, safe, stress-free, and predictable approach to quickly become debt-free and financially free on your own.

Let me show you the road less traveled so you can take charge and control of your own money—and stop playing the bankers, advisors, and financial-institutions game. The new model described in this book will eliminate your money stress and bring peace back into your life.

HOW TO CREATE PASSIVE INCOME FOR LIFE

This chapter is taken from my most recent book, entitled *The How-To Book on Dividend-Growth Investing—Create Generational Wealth and Passive Income for Life*. This book will show you a safe way to predictably earn enough passive income to replace your work income and lead to your financial independence.

A verse from the Eagles song "Already Gone" says "So often times it happens that we live our lives in chains, and we never even know we have the key." The key to your personal and financial independence is to get out of debt quickly and learn how to successfully invest on your own through undervalued blue-chip dividend-paying stocks.

The best investment strategies are always simple and easy to understand. My newest book, *The How To Book On Dividend Growth Investing* will show you step-by-step how to invest safely in the stock market on your own using undervalued dividend-paying stocks. It will show you how to select the best dividend stocks, give you specific examples of some of the best dividend companies, maximize your returns, minimize your taxes, and receive a never-ending flow of passive income. This becomes your new low-taxed pension plan for retirement without government control.

WHAT'S A DIVIDEND-GROWTH STOCK?

Put simply, a dividend-growth stock is a company with a proven track record of raising its dividend (a portion of corporate profits or cash reserves paid out to shareholders) year after year. High-quality dividend-growth companies typically dominate their industry, realizing steady profits and generating massive amounts of free cash flow. As a result, they're able to pay their shareholders from that cash in the form of dividends that increase every year . . . often rising faster than the rate of inflation.

The beauty of owning a stock like this is that, no matter what happens to its share price, if the company continues to grow its dividend, then we—as shareholders—stand to collect larger and larger payouts each year. That's why these stocks are so compelling:

you buy them when they're trading at a reasonable price, hold them, and then get showered with growing cash payouts for potentially decades to come!

Dividend investing is a slow, boring, and predictable way of becoming wealthy. Dividends create generational wealth. You will never worry about the stock price or fear the ups and downs of the market. With this strategy, you even hope the market goes down.

The greatest destroyers of investment wealth are expenses (advisor and mutual-fund fees), taxes, inflation, misinformation, not understanding the market, and your individual emotions (fear and greed).

When you learn to invest on your own, you will have no need for financial advisors, mutual-fund companies, or their high fees and commissions. Some of these "advisors" want to sell you complex, high-load mutual-fund investments that you don't understand. Their 1% to 3% commissions can result in a 25% to 80% lower return to you as the investor. Some advisors call themselves "wealth managers" because of the great wealth they create for themselves.

Depending on what state you live in, you could pay up to 50% in taxes, which might even get higher, depending on which party is in office. This is especially true when you must take the minimum distribution draw from your 401K or other retirement investments. The tax strategies in this book will show you how to reduce or eliminate all your taxes on your investments.

Investing in dividend-paying stocks is the greatest hedge against inflation and can be the best and safest place to put your money to beat inflation. Over the past 20 years, the inflation rate has been around 2.8%. In 2022, the inflation rate spiked to 9%, the highest inflation rate in 40 years, with no indication that it will fully subside soon.

You first need to learn how to invest on your own and know that the market always goes up over time. With a dividend investing strategy, you will care little about market-price fluctuations, recognizing that, when the market drops, you can take advantage of some incredible buying opportunities.

Your focus will be to maximize your passive income through dividend growth, while minimizing your taxes through monthly qualified dividends. You will see yourself as a long-term investor like Warren Buffett, whose financial success is powered by great dividend-paying companies that he will keep forever. You will learn to buy stocks when they are undervalued and receive great passive dividend income for life.

"If you don't find a way to make money while you sleep, you will work until you die."
— Warren Buffet

DIVIDEND EXAMPLE

The secret to successful investing is to have a step-by-step, simple, and safe long-term strategy that you thoroughly understand. With this investment strategy, you can retire a millionaire, but, more importantly, you will be able to *stay* a millionaire. My dividend-growth investment book will show you how to find and buy great undervalued dividend-paying companies (stocks) that will produce a consistent stream of minimally taxed passive income for the rest of your life. If you take the time to learn this simple system, you will learn to make money while you sleep so you will have the time to live the life of your dreams. The chart below will show you what is possible:

Portfolio starting with 3% dividend yield/15% annual dividend growth/10% annual equity growth with no additional money added in a tax-free Roth IRA

| One Time Starting Value | 10-YEAR RETURNS | | | | 20-YEAR RETURNS | | | |
| | No DRIP | | DRIP | | No DRIP | | DRIP | |
	Value	Ann Div Income	Value	Ann Div Income	Value	Ann Div Income	Value	Ann Div Income
$10,000	$26k	$1,200	$36k	$1,700	$67k	$4,900	$156k	$11,380
$50,000	$130k	$6,000	$180k	$8,400	$335k	$24.5k	$780k	$47.9k
$100,000	$260k	$12,000	$360k	$17,000	$670k	$49k	$1.56M	$114k

In this example, your portfolio starts with a 3% dividend yield. It assumes 15% annual dividend growth and 10% annual equity growth. Other than the one-time starting deposit in a tax-free Roth IRA, no further money is added.

If you did not reinvest any of the dividends during (No DRIP), a one-time initial $10,000 investment would have grown to $67,000 after 20 years, and you would receive $4,900 in annual dividend payments that year. If you did reinvest the dividends (DRIP), an initial $10,000 investment would be worth $156,000 at year 20, and your annual dividend income would be $11,380.

By comparison, if you started with a one-time investment of $100,000 with dividends reinvested (DRIP), then in 20 years, your portfolio would be worth $1.56 million, and you would be taking home $114,000 each year in passive income. This sounds crazy, but it is the power of compounding. If you held the stock for 30 years and got the same return, it would be worth $8,866,000 With an annual dividend income of $1,000,000 per year. This is true generational wealth.

Let's consider an example with an average investor who can put away $6,000 a year in their Roth IRA. Assume the same parameters with 3% dividend yield, 15% annual dividend growth, 10% annual equity growth, and automatically reinvest the dividends each year (DRIP). Their portfolio would be worth more than $4 million after 30 years, and they would be taking home, tax-free, $383,000 in dividends. In 40 years, their portfolio would be worth $36,822,000, with an annual dividend income of $6.5 million. That is real crazy.

Portfolio starting with 3% dividend yield/15% annual dividend growth/10% annual equity growth with $6,000 added money each year and dividends reinvested in a tax-free Roth IRA

	10-Year returns		20-Year returns		30-Year returns	
Starting	Value	Div Income	Value	Div Income	Value	Div Income
$6,000	$137,362	$6,427	$722,355	$52,720	$4,259,692	$484,902

These examples were derived using a representative dividend-focused portfolio. Later in this book is a list of companies that (as of the date printed) meet the recommended guidelines you will learn about. Keep in mind that there is never any guarantee when investing in the stock market. You can use the same online calculator to review any stock's performance for the past 20 years.

https://www.marketbeat.com/dividends/calculator/

There is also a great YouTube video to show how this concept works:

https://www.youtube.com/watch?v=luWaRka9LoY

MY INVESTMENT MENTOR

I learned this strategy from another dentist (we will call him "DDS"). He introduced me to the *IQT* newsletter to help me buy great dividend-paying companies when they are undervalued and what price to pay. In 2000, DDS started investing in dividend-paying stocks to prepare for his early retirement. DDS spent a lot of time researching the thousands of dividend-paying stocks in the market. In 2007 he was introduced to the *IQT* newsletter by a retired dentist and longtime user of the newsletter. He started to exclusively use the *IQT* newsletter for all his stock selection from the undervalued list. It was simple to use because they did all the research for him. He just enjoyed his life and never worried about what was happening in the market.

DDS retired debt-free at age 50 in 2008, with one portfolio of $1.5 million invested in the market. He was receiving more than $60,000 that year in dividends from one of his portfolios. The next year, just after he retired, his portfolio dropped 47% during the great recession. Surprisingly, his dividends increased in 2009 to $80,000. This was because he never sold his stocks—he continued to buy more undervalued blue-chip stocks on sale using the proceeds from his dividends. Also, when prices drop, many great companies increase their dividends to keep their investors.

Over the next 13 years, he lived on 85% of the dividends and reinvested the other 15% of the dividends back into his portfolio. As of December 2022, his portfolio was worth $10 million, and his annual dividend payout is now more than $360,000. This is an average annual dividend dividend-growth of 12.8% since 2009. Many of the companies listed in my dividend-growth book have even greater dividend growth. That is the power of continued increasing dividend growth!!!

During those years of investing in dividend stocks, DDS will receive an incredible 11.12% return on his dividends this year on his original cost basis of $3,046,000. His overall average annual return in his portfolio using the *IQT* newsletter from 2009 to 2022 was 19.4%, which was 4% higher than the S&P 500 average annual return of 15.3% without dividend reinvestment.

DDS loves this approach to investing because he does not need to do any research. He spends only about an hour once a month reading the *IQT* newsletter and puts in a limit or market buy order for a selected stock if the price is below the recommended price listed in the undervalued section of the newsletter.

He then sits back, relaxes, receives his dividends, and never worries about money or the ups and downs of the market. This once-a-month approach is like dollar-cost averaging, protecting you against your emotions and large swings in the market. He and his wife both have their own Schwab accounts and invest each month. She also does her own investments using the *IQT* newsletter. He now has a new updated airplane and they just bought a new home, paying in cash.

My friend told me that, in the past, like most investors, he had focused on the price of the stock. He has now realized that was the wrong number, as stock prices continually fluctuate up and down and are not that important to a long-term investor. DDS now knows the most important numbers to focus on are the dividend growth, dividend percentage yield, and the passive income returns he gets every month.

THE BUFFETT MINDSET

For those investors who are still working, you can reinvest 100% of your dividends plus invest added money each month, growing your dividend portfolio exponentially. Warren Buffett understands this concept well. His company Berkshire Hathaway does not pay dividends to their investors but reinvests all the dividends received from the companies under the umbrella of Berkshire Hathaway. Of the 48 securities within Berkshire Hathaway's holdings, 34 companies pay a regular dividend. In 2021, Buffett's Berkshire Hathaway annually receives $6.07 billion in dividends.

Warren Buffett, like DDS, rarely worries about the ups and downs in the market, knowing that the main goal is the returns on dividends. He plans to keep these companies forever and receive the continual cash flow of dividends. Like most dividend investors, he is hoping for a down market to buy great companies that have become undervalued.

Buffett understands that those companies that he owns under the umbrella of Berkshire Hathaway will continue to go up in time. He once said: "I never attempt to make money on the stock market. I buy on the assumption that they could close the market the next day and not reopen it for five years." It would not make a difference to long-term investors because they are in for the dividend passive income. If you want to know which blue-chip companies that Warren Buffett invests in, go to his annual report, and see how many Dividend Aristocrats he owns.

Once you read through the how-to book on dividend-growth investing and see how easy it is to invest on your own, and realize which companies are best to buy that will give you incredible returns, you can relax about your financial future, as you will be creating generational wealth.

ESTATE-PLANNING AND ASSET-PROTECTION CHECKLIST

More than 30% of the dentists I consult with do not have a will, power of attorney, or trust. Without these items, there is a great possibility that if something happens to you and your spouse, your drunken brother will take over all the money, spend it, and throw your kids out on the street. Think about it. Without a revocable living trust, your estate will go into probate, which makes all your assets public and is very expensive and emotionally draining to your heirs. It could take years before your estate is settled, thus depleting much of your estate's assets.

I was working with a 34-year-old dentist who had a very nice practice, a little girl, and one more child on the way. I told him to go to his local attorney and get these estate-planning documents drawn up. He said he would. Six months later, he was coming with his wife and team to one of my seminars in Seattle. During the flight, the plane had a landing-gear issue, and they thought they would have to make a crash landing in Seattle. Fortunately, they got the gear down and landed safely. At the meeting, I asked him, "Don't you feel better now that you have your asset-protection plan in place?" He sheepishly said, "I will get those things done as soon as I get back."

Find a local attorney, and get these things done now:

- Durable power of attorney for healthcare

- Durable power of attorney for finances

- Living will

- Standard will

- Revocable living trust

- Irrevocable trust

For a less-expensive approach you can also go to LegalZoom and set up one for as little as $250 with the help of its attorneys. http://www.legalzoom.com/living-trusts/living-trusts-overview.html

Make sure to update beneficiaries on all your banking and investment accounts. The beneficiaries get first claim, and those listed on the will are secondary.

Buy cheap term life insurance that will cover you until you're debt-free and you have created a portfolio of investments that can give you and your family passive income for life.

Should you buy or rent a home? Bottom line: Do not purchase a home until your student loans are all paid off and you have at least a 20% down payment. The average American moves every 7 years. By then, only 12% of the home is paid off with a 30-year mortgage. Then they get a new mortgage, starting all over again at

100%. With a $280,000 mortgage, they have paid $34,257 toward their mortgage and lost $90,569 to the bank in interest during those seven years. They also paid an additional 6% in sales commission ($16,800), $10,000 in home improvements, plus $4,000 in closing costs. The bottom line is that there was no increase in their net worth, and they will never, ever get out of debt.

If they stay in the home and choose to pay back the original $280,000 loan at 4.9% over the next 30 years, they will pay the $280,000 home price plus the $254,972 in interest, which equals $534,972 in after-tax money. I recommend that you never carry a mortgage larger than twice your gross income, and you should not spend more than 16% to 20% of your gross income on housing, including your mortgage payment, utilities, property tax, insurance, and maintenance. Buy a home that is just large enough for your family and one that you can afford to pay off in 7 to 10 years. Make sure that you get a mortgage that has no penalty or fee for paying it off early. If you pay off the $280,000 home in seven years, you would need to pay only $51,225 in interest and would save an additional $203,647 which would've gone to interest. Now you can use this money to invest in your retirement plan.

Remember: when buying a home over 30 years, most of the mortgage payments initially go to interest, and very little goes to the principal (ownership) to pay off the home. For the first 15 years it is just like renting, except you have all the additional property taxes, maintenance, and homeowner's insurance. Beyond that, in most cases, you can't even write off the interest on your taxes because they are less than the standard deduction. You are much better off renting until you have a 20% down payment (to eliminate the need for private mortgage insurance) and can plan to pay off the house in 7 to 10 years.

Focus all excess money on those payments, and don't dilute your extra money by paying into children's college funding or into your retirement unless it's matched by your employer. Once debt-free, then you can invest in your children's college funding and other retirement plans. When you buy a home, you now have real estate in your portfolio, and it becomes a form of forced savings, just like a long-term inflation-adjusted bond. And once paid off, that money which went to your mortgage payment now becomes like long-term dividends which can be invested more aggressively into the S&P 500 or total U.S. stock market. Your paid-off home also becomes a safety net from which equity can be used in emergencies through home-equity loans.

Unlike the dividends and interest from your investments, you don't have to pay taxes on inputted rent. This tax-free benefit is on top of the better-known tax breaks that home ownership enjoys, including the ability to take a tax deduction on the mortgage interest and property taxes, and to avoid capital gains tax on a big chunk of the profit when selling a home. In addition, when the market drops, you just don't go out and sell your home like many investors do with their stocks.

The choice between buying a home and renting one is among the biggest financial decisions that many adults make. I would recommend renting if you do not plan to live in the house for longer than seven years. Here is a calculator that uses the most important costs associated with buying a house and computes the equivalent monthly rent.

Get rid of private mortgage insurance (PMI). If you did not have a 20% down payment when you purchased your house, you had to buy PMI, or private mortgage insurance. This is very expensive and can cost you up to 1% of the loan amount annually. A $400,000 house will require $4,000 a year in insurance payments, or $333 in monthly payments. In accordance with the Homeowners Protection Act of 1998, your lender must terminate PMI on the date your loan balance is scheduled to reach 78% of the original value of your home (in other words, when your equity reaches 22%, provided you are current on your mortgage payments).

Call your lender and ask to cancel your PMI when you have paid down the mortgage balance to 80% of the home's original appraised value. You might have to write your lender a cancellation letter of the PMI. Accelerate your payments as fast as you can to eliminate the PMI and, once you've done this, you'll have an additional $333 a month to pay off your home early. https:/ www.investopedia.com/mortgage/ insurance/how-get-rid-pmi/

Chapter 5

Enjoy Life, Liberty, and the Pursuit of Happiness

Enjoying Good Health

ABOUT THREE YEARS AGO, I noticed that my computer IT guy had lost a considerable amount of weight. He was six-foot-two, and when I first met him, he weighed around 300 pounds. Within six months, he had dropped 100 pounds and now looked great. I was amazed because I disliked exercise and had always had trouble losing weight, so I asked him what his secret was.

He told me that weight loss was pretty much 90% diet and 10% exercise. He said he changed his eating habits and moved to a high-fat, low-carbohydrate, ketogenic method of eating. He recommended a site called Dietdoctor.com, which was founded in 2011 and has more than 55,000 members worldwide, making it the largest low-carb site in the world. It is filled with many articles, experts, videos, and low-carb recipes.

At that time, I was five-foot-six and weighed about 200 pounds, with a beautiful pot belly. Within three months of taking his advice, I lost more than 35 pounds and have maintained my weight at 165 pounds for the past 3 years. I walk a couple of miles once a week and do some weightlifting two times a week to keep my muscle tone. I take multivitamins, vitamin D, magnesium, and fish oil. I can now sleep 8 hours a night, and I feel better than I have for years.

Another great website to help transform your health is http://drhyman.com/. Dr. Mark Hyman is an American physician and a *New York Times* bestselling author. He is the founder and medical director of the Ultra Wellness Center and director of the Cleveland Clinical Center for Functional Medicine.

CREATING GREAT RELATIONSHIPS

Warren Buffett gives the following advice: *"Be around people that you admire and enjoy. They usually have an upbeat attitude about life, they're humorous, have integrity and are generous people who are thinking about what they can do for you. These qualities that you admire are not innate at birth, and you can acquire them. Then there are those negative qualities that turn you off in people who always need to be right and that you don't enjoy being with. You can choose what person you want to be, so why not choose the person you admire? Take your five best friends, mentors or your heroes, and write down the qualities that you like about them. Incorporate these qualities in your life, and eliminate the qualities of the people that turn you off. It's that simple. It is important to work with people in your life, and you will get the best out of people if they like you. You need to develop these habits now. Incorporate the great qualities now and eliminate the bad qualities, and you will have an incredible life. Choose your heroes very carefully because they will define you. You are one of your children's favorite heroes."*

Buffett also said that the secret to long-lasting relationships is low expectations. A friend told me that relationships improved immensely when you give up the need to be right. My wife, Nancy, and I were married in 1969. We have 5 children and 13 grand-children. We have had our ups and downs, but we are very supportive of each other. And if she has a problem that I know I can fix immediately, I listen intently and never offer advice. (There is a great and funny YouTube clip called *"It's Not About the Nail"* that makes this point very clear.)

One last comment: I would never be in a relationship that is toxic or does not add true meaning to my life. Sadly, this toxicity could be from parents who are always judgmental and critical of you. Tell any toxic person that if they continue to be judgmental or critical, you will not be seeing them. I give you permission to take care of yourself first, or else you will not be good to anyone else. Think about what you are teaching your children about the type of relationship they should be in.

LIVING IN THE MOMENT

When asked, who is the most important person in your life right now, most people would think about their children or their spouse. Because we can only live in the moment, the most important people in your life right now are the people you are with right now. When you understand this, you will focus and enjoy those relationships at much deeper level. Most people spend too much of their time thinking about or worrying about the past or the future which keeps them from truly enjoying the present.

In his book, *Way of The Peaceful Warrior*, Dan Millman *reminds us that the time is now, the place is here. Stay in the present. You can do nothing to change the past, and the future will never come exactly as you plan or hope for. Life comes to us in waves. We cannot control the waves, but we can learn to surf. Apply the law of surrender, the law of acceptance. The secret is to take action and make use of that moment and learn to enjoy the ride.*

In a recent interview he shared three lessons: *First, trust in your process of your life unfolding and not comparing you or your life to other people. Second, have the courage to live as if everything that happens is for our highest good and learning. Third, remember your innate worth as a human being and treat yourself kindly with compassion as you would treat others.*

CREATING LOVE IN YOUR LIFE

Love is that special feeling we get when we have a connection with people and things in our life. It is created when we initiate and give love to people and things. Somebody could love us, and yet we may not feel anything. But we always feel love when we are loving others. We are fortunate to be in a profession where we can love our patients, our team, what we do, and especially our family. This doesn't apply only to loving people but also to things in our lives such as a good movie, a book, a special mug, and other things we go back to and create that feeling of love. Like the movie, *Love Actually* is all around us.

LETTING GO OF ISSUES AND EMOTIONAL PAIN FROM YOUR PAST

When I was three years old, my mother divorced my father, and he moved to another city. My mother had to go back to school to get her degree, and my brothers and I lived with my grandmother for the next five years. At that young age I subconsciously blamed myself for their divorce because if I could had been a better little boy, this would not have happened. I carried this shame and pain through adulthood hoping that no one would find out how bad I was. I subconsciously stuffed this emotional pain and started to feel from my brain, not my heart, where there was no pain. This inability to feel deep emotions affected many in my personal and business relationships.

I can easily understand why many men are not emotional. Once I addressed the issue and let go of this emotional pain, which can be easily done with proper techniques, my life and I became more emotionally alive and peaceful. Many people carry deeply embedded emotional pain from their past that affects and controls their lives. This could be from abandonment (divorce), which I experienced, sexual abuse, not being wanted; there are many more. One group I worked with who are exceptionally good in helping individuals to identify, address, and let go of these issues is Legacy Life Consulting. Contact them at: https://www.legacylifeconsulting.com/ David Stamation (208) 946-3894.

YOU NEED TO TAKE CARE OF YOURSELF FIRST

Many people feel they are serving others by giving away all their time and energies helping others, but by doing so they are not taking care of themselves, leaving them feeling exhausted, frustrated, and angry. This is especially true with women. The sad part is, they could better serve and help others if they took care of their own needs first. They need to set time aside just for themselves to love and nurture themselves first, and they will feel much better, less resentful, and happier as they serve others. The magic phrase that they need to use more often is "No—I cannot do that. Thanks for asking."

TEACHING YOUR CHILDREN ABOUT FINANCES

Mahatma Gandhi was asked what his message to the world was. He said, "My life is my message." Teach your children the satisfaction of being a saver instead of a spender. You need to show them the satisfaction of accomplishment and doing a job well done. Be the example for them of how they can find fun and joy in everything they do, instead of teaching them duty, respon- sibility, and that you must work hard for a living.

Teach your children to understand the ideas in this book. Help your children find a job so that they can learn to love work, save, and be disciplined with their money. Show them the power of getting out of debt and creating and funding their own Roth IRA. Teach them the value of money and the feeling of freedom associated with being debt-free.

STOP COMPLAINING

Half of the people think you deserve what you get, and the other half don't care. Kendrick Mercer shared a story with me after his three-month sailing from California to Lahaina, Maui. His trip was an incredible adventure, with beautiful sunny days, stormy weather, moonbows at night, and wonderful solitude. After arriving in Lahaina, he took a plane to Honolulu. He was enjoying the view over the ocean while a lady sitting next to him was complaining to him about her life, children, and husband. During the break in her conversation, he looked at her and said, "Let us play a game. Let us pretend the plane breaks right in half, and we are all going to die. All you see in front of you is blue sky. We have two choices: we can grab on to the armrest in terror and think about all the things we didn't do in our life, or we can calmly unbuckle our seatbelts, stand up, jump forward, and fly for the rest of our lives." She did not say much after that but gave him a big hug at the end of the flight. Why not live our life in gratitude and enjoy every moment?

HOW DO WE DEFINE SUCCESS?

This can be different for each one of us. For me, it is about loving what I do each day, being at peace in my life, being in good health, having time to be with and enjoy the people I love, being debt-free, having enough money that I don't worry about money anymore, and having the time and resources to make a difference in the world around me. Others may define success as being the best businessman, making a lot of money, having time to do missionary work, retiring at age 55, having $2 million in the bank—the list goes on. This book is not meant to define your success but to show you how to have enough time and money to make choices in your life that are right for you. *It is not about making a living. It is about making a life worth living.*

French writer François-René de Chateaubriand (1768 to 1848) said, *"A master in the art of living draws no sharp distinction between his work and his play; his labor and his leisure; his mind and his body; his education and his recreation. He hardly knows which is which; he simply pursues his vision of excellence through whatever he is doing and leaves others to determine whether he is working or playing. To himself, he always appears to be doing both."*

HOW MUCH IS ENOUGH?

If you are like most people in the world, one bowl of rice a day would be enough. Here in America, we think in terms of economic freedom. In my past book *Time and Money,* I define economic freedom as the day you have accumulated enough safe, liquid assets that can reproduce your lifestyle income (the amount of money it takes to maintain your lifestyle), with safeguards against inflation, for the rest of your life without touching the principal. This will vary by individual, but once you are debt-free, you could reach that point in five to seven years, simply by following the recommendations in this book.

MAKE A DIFFERENCE IN THE WORLD

There is a difference between success and significance. One of the great advantages of having more time and more money is the ability to make a difference in the lives of people in the world around us. One reason I enjoy going into the office two days a week is that I can create abundance to share with others. Because I am debt-free, each year, I significantly donate to many great causes, including the Union Gospel Mission dental clinic for our street people, Safe Place for battered women, the food banks, a dental assisting program, my church, AAE Foundation, and various other causes that make a difference in the world around me. I believe that this brings even more abundance into my life. Even though you are working on paying off debt, donate either your time or money to an important cause. This will make a difference in your life and those you help.

THE $2 FREEDOM AND HAPPINESS BILL

I love giving out $2 bills as a reminder of our freedom in the United States. This $2 bill is the only piece of U.S. currency that depicts the same person on the front and standing on the back. On the front of the bill, we see Thomas Jefferson, the third president of the United States. Then we turn the bill over and see him signing the Declaration of Independence. The people standing around the table are the committee who wrote the declaration. The main author is Thomas Jefferson (the tall person in the center). The person standing on the far left is John Adams, the second president of the United States.

John Adams and Thomas Jefferson had a few things in common: They were both presidents and were the only presidents who signed the Declaration of Independence. They both died on July 4, within three hours of each other, exactly 50 years after they signed the Declaration of Independence.

In those days, the average man lived to 35 years of age. Adams was 90, and Jefferson was 83 on the day they died. I believe the reason they lived two to three generations beyond the average man is that they were both highly motivated to instill and imprint the ideals of freedom and independence into our American culture. They lived with a purpose.

This is what makes the United States one of the freest countries in the world; we can work and live anywhere we want in this
country. We are free to be in any mutual relationship we want
and to leave it if it is toxic (a relationship where you will never
grow and are always being put down).

Sadly, most Americans don't know they are free. Many feel
trapped in their lives, business, jobs, and relationships. They
feel angry, controlled, frustrated, anxious, or sad. These feelings come from a place of fear—many people fear change and
have one foot in and one foot out of their choices (relationships
or jobs). These feelings immediately disappear when the person
acts, after choosing to change, or by putting "both feet in and
out" of their choice.

The $2 bill reminds us of our choice to be free, independent,
and happy. The secret of happiness is in three choices. Any time
you feel upset, angry, or trapped, there is something in your life

that you are not accepting. The courage to make one of these three choices will give you back your freedom and peace of mind. The choices are as follows:

1. You can change your situation (relationship or work), which takes courage as you face and conquer your fears. For example, if someone is always judgmental or critical of you and this is a deal-breaker, then you can tell them that behavior is no longer acceptable to you and that, if they continue, you will leave the relationship. If they stop this unacceptable behavior, then you will stay and be at peace. If not, you choose number two.

2. You can leave the situation (i.e., relationship or work).

3. If you can't change the situation or you choose not to leave the situation, then you can stay and accept the "what is" of the situation and be totally at peace with the situation because it is your choice. We need to change: "Why is this happening to me?" to "Why is this happening **for** me?"

Final Thoughts

CREATE A PRACTICE YOU LOVE. Let a practice management coach help you become much more profitable so you can focus that money on debt reduction and your financial freedom. Once you are debt free, learn how to invest on your own in great dividend-growth companies. Many business owners I coach complain about some of the people they work with who make them miserable. I tell them to go back to their office and tell the owner to fire those people. Then I remind them that *they are the owner.* Most people forget that they can make their business exactly what they want it to be. They have the canvas and the brush.

Stop listening to the news and worrying about what's happening in the market or the country. This is just noise. That's it. Now, enjoy your life, be grateful, and spend the rest of your money on things that add meaning to your life. This leads to financial freedom and a life of self-integrity and peace.

Economic peace of mind is more than just financial freedom. In fact, we can experience economic peace of mind long before we reach financial freedom. *Once we have a solid guide in place for achieving financial freedom, we can let go of our anxiety about money and live as if it has already happened.* With this newfound peace of mind, we can truly enjoy life in the moment because we are secure in what we have, and we know that we can deal with any life challenge.

Now we can face life with joy and excitement once we have a vision and a beautiful story for our lives. With this book, each of us can claim both financial freedom *and* economic and personal peace of mind. "Being happy is a choice."

Praise for

The Dentist's Guide to Creating Personal and Financial Freedom

Dr. Ace Goerig is a genius when it comes to unlocking the keys to finances and happiness in life! He loves sharing his easy-to-implement secrets of contentment, enthusiam, and living the good life . . . all at the same time. For decades he has studied burned-out employers/employees in the workforce. From the CEO/owner to the entry-level employees, workers are simply tired of the noose around their necks called "debt."

We all know that debt reduction at a fast pace is the key to this thirst for "working because we love it" versus hating for Monday to roll around to go back to the paycheck-to-paycheck existence.

Ace's book outlines exactly what others can do to achieve this ravenous happiness in life. There are several key elements: Live below your means early on; pay yourself first each payday; be the most ethical person you know; hire experts to provide the growth in your business that compounds your net by tens of thousands per month. This not only pays down the debt quickly, it allows you to work because you "get to" rather than "have to." That, folks, is pure happiness.

—**Linda Miles, Founder/CEO**, Linda Miles & Associates; Founder, Speaking Consulting Network

Every dentist should keep this book bedside and read and re-read it. The advice is sound and easy to understand and implement. I consider Ace Goerig as a combination of John Bogle and Warren Buffett for dentists who want a secure financial future.

—**Dan Solin**, Author of the Smartest series of investing books

Ace has created a blueprint that has been found tried and true thousands of times. You are fortunate that you don't have to reinvent the wheel or spend one more day struggling only to find another strategy that does not work. This is a playbook for success in life in which Ace outlines a concise, consistent financial plan for Dentists that works.

—**Michael Abernathy DDS**, Founder of Summit Practice Solutions

A superb book! Dr. Goerig demonstrates the keys to happiness and financial success. The core of his message is to become financially free while enjoying your life. Money in and of itself will not make you happy but having enough money to not worry about money allows you to develop your passions. Build enough wealth through conservative proven investments, get out of debt, gain perspective, and then use most of your time cultivating a life that is real, a life based on what you want, not what your parents or society tells you to be. Follow his advice, all of it, and I assure you that you will be 1,000% better for it!

—**Alex Nottingham**, JD, MBA, Founder & CEO of All-Star Dental Academy

I've known Ace for 35 years and he has always been focused on value, quality, self-improvement, and mentoring others. This book is a continuation of those attributes and gives the reader the skills and knowledge to live a life of peace, joy, hope, contentment, achievement, and financial freedom. By putting his principles into action, you will be able to claim "victory," and that success will spread to your office staff, your patients, and, most importantly, your family.

—**James C. Kulild, DDS, MS,** Past President, American Association of Endodontists, Diplomate, American Board of Endodontics, Professor Emeritus, Department of Endodontics UMKC School of Dentistry

As a dentist in practice for 15 years, I have often struggled with who to believe when it came to investing and a financial philosophy for life. I often was torn between what was the best way to live and spend and save. It is such an important topic with so many different opinions on the "right way." I found Ace 5 years ago, and he and his philosophy have totally changed my life, and all the secrets are contained in this short book. I truly believe that this is the "right" way and have made a commitment to read this book at the beginning of each year to remind myself. Thank you, Ace. I am now living a more meaningful, happy, purposeful, almost debt-free life because of you and your relentless passion to help others.

—**Derek White DDS**, Madison, MS

This book is one of the most comprehensive and compelling publications on the subject that I have experienced. It's uniqueness and what differentiates it from others is that it specifically addresses the lifelong needs and goals of dentists everywhere—issues and subject matter certainly not taught in our nation's dental schools. This book is a terrific read for all of us at any stage of our career, to and through retirement.

—**Hugh Habas DDS**, New Jersey national presenter on practice management

Here it is in a wonderful, compact nutshell—the "crux" of the Ace Goerig philosophy of practice, personal finance, and life boiled down to this beautiful guide for happiness in our practice and personal life! Why "recreate the wheel" when you have the best practice-management mentor generously sharing his experiences and wisdom to us for a life filled with peace, joy, and fulfillment? This book is a must-read for all dentists and gives us life skills to share with our loved ones, too!

—**Richard C. Wittenauer, DDS**, diplomate, ABE, California